Knits for Kitties

Knits for Kitties

25 knitting patterns for making cat toys

Sara Elizabeth Kellner

KNITS FOR KITTIES
A QUARTO BOOK

Published in 2016 by
New Burlington Books
6 Blundell Street
London N7 9BH

ISBN: 978-0-85762-154-2

QUAR.KCCT

Conceived, designed and produced by
Quarto Publishing plc
The Old Brewery
6 Blundell Street
London N7 9BH
www.quartoknows.com

Senior editor: Lily de Gatacre
Art editor and designer: Jackie Palmer
Photographers: Liz Coleman, Phil Wilkins and Laura Forrester
Illustrator: Kuo Kang Chen
Proofreader: Liz Jones
Indexer: Helen Snaith
Art director: Caroline Guest

Creative director: Moira Clinch
Publisher: Paul Carslake

Colour separation in Singapore
by Pica Digital Pte Limited
Printed in China
by Toppan Leefung Pte Limited

10 9 8 7 6 5 4 3 2 1

CONTENTS

WELCOME TO MY WORLD

Welcome to the world of Rabbit Hole Knits. I used to say that I would never knit a toy. The only ones that seemed popular at that time were monsters or just looked too 'cartoony' to me. Most of them were also knitted flat, which means lots of piecing together and sewing up at the end. It didn't occur to me that I could design a toy of my own, make it look realistic and use any method of construction I liked.

Then, one day, I wanted to knit an animal to give as a gift and because I couldn't find a pattern that appealed to me, I sat down to create one of my own. It was a sheep, knitted in the round, and before the day was over the pattern was finished. In fact, the designing process was so exciting and rewarding to me that ever since that day, I've hardly stopped!

When you look at my designs, I think it's easy to see what inspires me: children and animals, especially the common house cat! Tortoiseshells are my favourite cats; I think I've always had one. These days my knitting companion is Miss Sunny Dupree.

She's happy both indoors and outside in the wild, wild west (my front garden) hunting grasshoppers and chasing butterflies. And actually, when it came to choosing which designs would be in this book, I left it up to her. If Sunny has ever chased it, batted it, stalked it, pounced on it or sniffed it – I re-created it for this book.

If you've never tried knitting in the round on double-pointed needles before, these little patterns are the perfect place to start. Most of them can be completed in just a couple of hours, and with yarn you already have in your stash.

It's my sincere hope that you will have as much fun knitting these cat toys as your kitty will have playing with them!

Sara Elizabeth Kellner

TOY PATTERNS

Coming up in this chapter are twenty-five projects for you to try. Each project is marked as either beginner, intermediate or advanced, so you can choose one that suits your skill level. Or just pick the design that you think will most delight your cat, and get knitting.

Skill level: Advanced

There's a mouse in the house!

What cat can resist the lure of a little mouse? Keep your kitty entertained for hours with these knitted creations. Fill them with catnip and the hunt is on!

METHOD

Work begins at the neckline.

With colour A, CO 13 sts onto 3 3.5 mm dpns. Join in the round and work the rounds below:

Round 1: K all sts.

Round 2: M1, k12, m1, k1. (15 sts)

Rounds 3–4: K all sts.

Round 5: M1, k14, m1, k1. (17 sts)

Rounds 6–7: K all sts.

Round 8: M1, k1, m1, k14, [m1, k1] twice. (21 sts)

Rounds 9–12: K all sts.

Round 13: [K1, k2tog] 3 times, k3, [ssk, k1] 3 times. (15 sts)

Round 14: K all sts.

Round 15: [K2tog] 3 times, k3, [ssk] 3 times. (9 sts)

Round 16: K all sts.

Round 17: [K2tog] twice, k1, [ssk] twice. (5 sts)

Round 18: K2tog, k1, ssk. (3 sts)

Round 19: K1, slip that st to the other side of your dpn. Slip the two remaining sts (beginning with the last st in round) onto the same dpn as the knitted st. You will now have three sts on one dpn.

Cut colour A. Switch to colour B and 2.75 mm dpns. Work a 3-stitch I-cord (see page 96) for 6.5 cm (2½ inches). On the next row, k2tog, k1, then work a 2-stitch I-cord for an additional 2.5 cm (1 inch). Cut yarn, thread through remaining 2 live sts and pull tightly closed. Stuff body firmly and weave in loose ends.

continued on page 13

SUPPLIES

- Aran weight yarn in two colours:
  Colour A (body and head): 9 m (10 yards)
  Colour B (tail, legs and ears): 9 m (10 yards)
- Scrap of black yarn for eyes (optional)
- 3.5 mm double-pointed needles
- 2.75 mm double-pointed needles
- Darning needle
- Choice of stuffing (hollowfibre filling or catnip)

Size: 7.5 cm (3 inches) long (without tail)

Head

Sts are now picked up in the original CO sts to shape the head. With colour A and 3.5 mm dpns, begin at the first CO st and PU 13 sts: 1 in each CO st (see page 96). Then work the rounds below.

Note: Rows 2–4 are short rows worked back and forth (not in the round). (See page 97 for instructions on working short rows.) Stuffing can be added to the head as you go, or after round 8 and before closing.

Round 1: K all sts.

Row 2: K2, wt, p4, wt, k2.

Row 3: K3, wt, p6, wt, k3.

Row 4: K4, wt, p8, wt, k4.

Round 5: [K1, k2tog] 4 times, k1. (9 sts)

Round 6: K all sts.

Round 7: [K2tog] 4 times, k1. (5 sts)

Round 8: K all sts.

Cut yarn, thread through remaining live sts and pull tightly closed. Weave in all loose ends, using them to darn any holes. Embroider eyes using black yarn if desired.

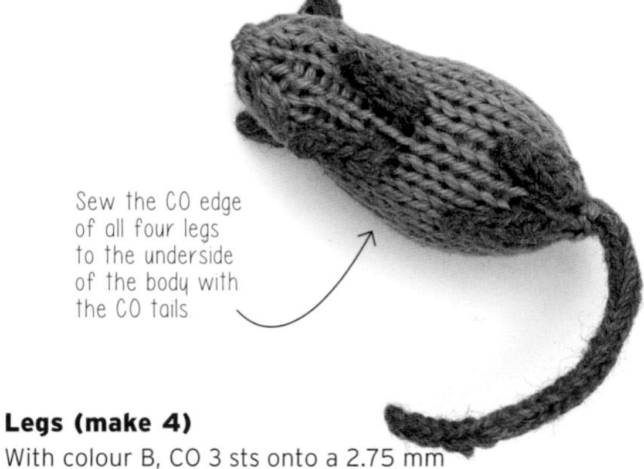

Sew the CO edge of all four legs to the underside of the body with the CO tails.

Legs (make 4)

With colour B, CO 3 sts onto a 2.75 mm dpn and work 4 rows of a 3-stitch I-cord. Cut yarn, thread through live sts, pull tightly closed and weave in loose end. Sew the CO edge of all four legs to the underside of the body with the CO tails, as pictured above.

Ears (make 2)

With colour B, CO 5 sts onto a 2.75 mm dpn and work the following rows back and forth:

Row 1: Sl1 purlwise, p4.

Row 2: Sl1 knitwise, k4.

Row 3: Sl1 purlwise, p4.

Weave in the CO tail onto the P side. Cut yarn, thread through 5 remaining live sts. Pull closed to cinch bottom of ear together; sew this end to the head.

Embroider eyes to bring your mouse to life.

Desilu's doughnut

Skill level: Advanced

This fun, cute design is the perfect way to give your kitty a sweet treat! Stuff these doughnuts with catnip and she really will find them irresistable.

SUPPLIES

- Aran weight yarn: 18.25 m (20 yards)
- Scraps of yarn in other colours (for sprinkles)
- 3.5 mm double-pointed needles
- Darning needle
- Choice of stuffing (hollowfibre filling or catnip)

Size: 7.5 cm (3 inches) diameter

METHOD

CO 12 sts onto 3 dpns. Join in the round and work the rounds below:

Round 1: K all sts.

Round 2: K4, wt, p8, wt, k4. (See page 97 for instructions on working short rows.)

Repeat Rounds 1–2 21 more times, or until the two ends meet (the number of repeats may vary slightly depending on your yarn).

If you wish, wraps can be picked up and knitted along with the sts on the plain knit round in order to minimise holes created by the wraps and turns.

Cast off all sts. Stuff your doughnut and sew the two sides together. Embroider on multi-coloured sprinkles or leave plain.

A teddy of his own

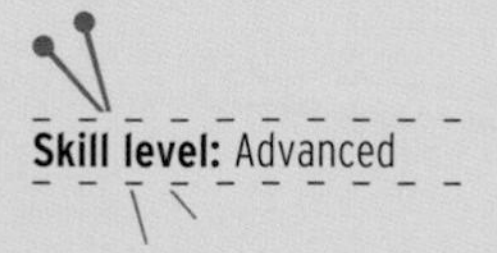

Make your little friend his very own teddy bear companion. You can play around with the design and colour of Teddy's outfit, and it can be a great way to use up little scraps of leftover yarn.

METHOD

Body
Work begins at neckline.

With colour A, CO 18 sts onto 3 dpns. Join in the round and work the rounds below:

Round 1: K all sts.

Round 2: K2, m1, k1, m1, k2, m1, k1, m1, k5, m1, k1, m1, k2, m1, k1, m1, k3. (26 sts)

Round 3: K all sts.

Round 4: K3, m1, k1, m1, k4, m1, k1, m1, k7, m1, k1, m1, k4, m1, k1, m1, k4. (34 sts)

Round 5: K all sts.

Round 6: K4, m1, k1, m1, k6, m1, k1, m1, k9, m1, k1, m1, k6, m1, k1, m1, k5. (42 sts)

Round 7: K all sts.

Round 8: K5, m1, k1, m1, k8, m1, k1, m1, k11, m1, k1, m1, k8, m1, k1, m1, k6. (50 sts)

Round 9: K all sts.

Round 10: K7, slip next 11 (arm) sts onto a piece of scrap yarn, k14, slip next 11 (arm) sts onto a piece of scrap yarn, k7. (28 sts)

Round 11: K all sts.

Round 12: K6, m1, k2, m1, k12, m1, k2, m1, k6. (32 sts)

Rounds 13-16: K all sts.

Round 17: P all sts.

Round 18: K all sts.

Round 19: P all sts.

Cut colour A.

Legs
Join colour B and work the following rounds:

Rounds 1-4: K all sts. (32 sts)

Round 5: K16, slip next 16 sts onto a piece of scrap yarn, CO 2 sts to end and divide sts onto 3 dpns (6 sts on each). Join in the round and work the following rounds:

SUPPLIES

- Aran weight yarn in three colours:
  Colour A (shirt): 9 m (10 yards)
  Colour B (trousers): 7.3 m (8 yards)
  Colour C (hands, feet and head): 9 m (10 yards)
- Scraps of black yarn (for eyes, nose and mouth)
- Piece of additional scrap yarn
- 3.5 mm double-pointed needles
- Darning needle
- Choice of stuffing (hollowfibre filling or catnip)

Size: 18 cm (7 inches) tall

Rounds 6-15: K all sts. (18 sts)

Cut colour B.

Join colour C and continue with the rounds below:

Rounds 16-21: K all sts.

Round 22: [K2tog] 9 times. (9 sts)

Cut yarn, thread through remaining live sts and pull closed. Weave in all loose ends. Place 16 sts from the scrap yarn onto 3 dpns and knit across them. CO 2 new sts to end, divide sts onto 3 dpns (6 sts on each) and join in the round.

Repeat Rounds 6-22 above.

Cut yarn, thread through remaining live sts and pull closed. Weave in all loose ends.

continued on next page

Customise your teddy's outfit with different colours and patterns.

On a stripy jumper, make sure the slight step between rounds is hidden at the back.

Arms
Place 11 arm sts from one of the pieces of scrap yarn onto 2 dpns. With colour A, PU 3 sts from underarm (see page 96). Join in the round and work the following rounds:

Rounds 1–5: K all sts. (14 sts)

Cut colour A.

Join colour C and continue with the rounds below:

Rounds 6–11: K all sts.

Round 12: [K2tog] 7 times. (7 sts)

Cut yarn, thread through remaining live sts and pull closed. Weave in all loose ends. Place 11 arm sts from the other piece of scrap yarn onto 2 dpns and PU 3 sts from second underarm, repeat Rounds 1–12 above for the second arm. Darn any holes underneath arms.

To seam the hole between the legs, turn your Teddy inside out and hold the sides of the hole together. Make one seam from front to back (or back to front). Turn right side out again. Stuff the body through the neck opening.

Head
With colour C, begin at the first CO st (centre of your Teddy's back) and PU 18 sts: 1 in each of the original CO sts. Join in the round and work the following rounds:

Round 1: K all sts.

Round 2: K3, m1, k2, m1, k8, m1, k2, m1, k3. (22 sts)

Round 3: K all sts.

Round 4: K4, m1, k2, m1, k10, m1, k2, m1, k4. (26 sts)

Round 5: K all sts.

Round 6: K5, m1, k2, m1, k12, m1, k2, m1, k5. (30 sts)

Round 7: K all sts.

Round 8: K6, m1, k2, m1, k14, m1, k2, m1, k6. (34 sts)

Rounds 9–13: K all sts.

Round 14: K6, ssk, k2, k2tog, k10, ssk, k2, k2tog, k6. (30 sts)

Round 15: K5, ssk, k2, k2tog, k8, ssk, k2, k2tog, k5. (26 sts)

Round 16: K4, ssk, k2, k2tog, k6, ssk, k2, k2tog, k4. (22 sts)

Round 17: K3, ssk, k2, k2tog, k4, ssk, k2, k2tog, k3. (18 sts)

Round 18: K2, ssk, k2, k2tog k2, ssk, k2, k2tog, k2. (14 sts)

Round 19: K1, ssk, k2, k2tog, ssk, k2, k2tog, k1. (10 sts)

Cut yarn and thread through remaining live sts; stuff head before pulling closed. Weave in loose ends.

Snout
With colour C, CO 6 sts onto 3 dpns. Join in the round and work the rounds below:

Round 1: K all sts.

Round 2: [M1, k1] 6 times. (12 sts)

Round 3: K all sts.

Round 4: [M1, k2] 6 times. (18 sts)

Cast off all sts. Seam to face, adding stuffing just before finishing.

Ears (make 2)
With colour C, CO 12 sts onto 3 dpns. Join in the round and work the rounds below:

Rounds 1–3: K all sts.

Round 4: [K2tog] 6 times. (6 sts)

Cut yarn, thread through remaining live sts and pull closed. Seam to head unstuffed.

Embroider nose, mouth and eyes.

Caterpillar crazy

Skill level: Beginner

This cute creepy-crawly is quick and easy to make but you can add so much fun detail. Perfect for your adventurous pet to stalk and hunt in the back garden.

SUPPLIES

- Aran weight yarn in three colours:
  Colour A (body): 6.4 m (7 yards)
  Colour B (stripes): 4.5 m (5 yards)
  Colour C (dots): 1 m (1 yard)
- 3.5 mm double-pointed needles
- Darning needle

Size: 11.5 cm (4½ inches) long

Pattern notes:

- Select a heavier aran weight yarn over a lighter one for this pattern.
- In order to minimise the appearance of colour changes, simply bring the new colour over the old one each time you switch to a new colour.
- Do not stuff your caterpillar.

METHOD

Work begins at head.

With colour A, CO 6 sts onto 3 dpns. Join in the round and work the rounds below:

Round 1 (colour A): K all sts.

Round 2 (colour B): K1, m1, k4, m1, k1. (8 sts)

Rounds 3-6 (colour A): K all sts.

Round 7 (colour B): K all sts.

Rounds 8-11 (colour A): K all sts.

Rounds 12-31: Repeat Rounds 7-11 four more times, then work the following rounds:

Round 32 (colour B): K1, k2tog, k2, ssk, k1. (6 sts)

Rounds 33-34 (colour A): K all sts.

Cut yarn, thread through remaining live sts and pull closed. Weave in both loose ends.

- With colour C, embroider four small dots on each of the colour B stripes, as pictured above.
- Make two small antennae with colour B (see page 102).
- To create the separate segments of your caterpillar, begin by cutting six pieces of colour B yarn, each one about 20 cm (8 inches) long. Tie one of them loosely around your caterpillar between two of the colour B stripes, centre it, then pull tightly to cinch. Tie a second knot on top of the first one. Thread one of the ends into a darning needle, insert down into your caterpillar at the location of the knot, then up through the body close to one of the colour B stripes; cut yarn.

Repeat with the other end.

Repeat with the five remaining pieces of yarn.

Skill level: Advanced

Bye-bye birdie

If your cat loves to jump around, this little hummingbird will be right up his alley. Dangle the bird from a strand of yarn and make him swoop and fly around the room.

METHOD

Body
Work begins at neckline.

With colour A, CO 9 sts onto 3 3.5 mm dpns. Join in the round and work the rounds below:

Round 1: K all sts.

Round 2: [M1, k3] 3 times. (12 sts)

Cut colour A. Join colour B.

Round 3: K all sts.

Round 4: K5, m1, k2, m1, k5. (14 sts)

Round 5: K all sts.

Round 6: K5, m1, k4, m1, k5. (16 sts)

Rounds 7–9: K all sts.

Round 10: K5, ssk, k2, k2tog, k5. (14 sts)

Round 11: K4, ssk, k2, k2tog, k4. (12 sts)

Round 12: K3, ssk, k2, k2tog, k3. (10 sts)

Round 13: K2, ssk, k2, k2tog, k2. (8 sts)

Rounds 14–16: K all sts.

Round 17: K2, ssk, k2tog, k2. (6 sts)

Rounds 18–20: K all sts.

Cut yarn, thread through remaining live sts and pull closed. Weave in loose ends. Stuff body firmly from CO sts to about Round 10 (where decreases begin). The tail is left unstuffed and flattened.

Note: The side of the body with the increases and decreases on it will be the underside (belly) of your hummingbird.

continued on page 25

SUPPLIES

- Aran weight yarn in three colours:
  - **Colour A** (breast): 1.8 m (2 yards)
  - **Colour B** (body, head and wings): 9 m (10 yards)
  - **Colour C** (throat): 1.8 m (2 yards)
- Scraps of black yarn (for eyes)
- 3.5 mm double-pointed needles
- 2.75 mm double-pointed needles
- Darning needle
- Choice of stuffing (hollowfibre filling or catnip)

Size: 10 cm (4 inches) long

Note: Colour changes described in this pattern are for a three-colour bird with the above specifications. Of course, any number of colours and combinations can be used to make your own hummingbird.

Head
With colour C and 3.5 mm dpns, begin at the first CO st (centre of your bird's back) and PU 9 sts: 1 in each of the original CO sts (see page 96). Work the rounds below:

Rounds 1-2: K all sts.

Cut colour C. Join colour B.

Round 3: K all sts.

Round 4: K2, wt, p4, wt, k2. (See page 97 for instructions on working short rows.)

Round 5: K2, wt, p4, wt, k2.

Round 6: K2, wt, p4, wt, k2.

Round 7: K all sts. (9 sts)

Stuff the head at this point.

Switch to 2.75 mm dpns on the following round, and for the remainder of the head and beak.

Round 8: K2, ssk, k1, k2tog, k2. (7 sts)

Round 9: K1, ssk, k1, k2tog, k1. (5 sts)

Round 10: Ssk, k1, k2tog (work these all on 1 dpn). (3 sts)

Slide sts to the other side of the dpn (as with an I-cord), then k2tog, k1. Work a 2-stitch I-cord (see page 96) for 3 additional rows. Cut yarn, thread through live sts and weave in end. Loose ends can be used to darn holes in neck and head.

Right wing
With 3.5 mm dpns, sts are now picked up along the back of your hummingbird to make the wings.

Beginning just below the last round of colour A (Round 3), and with the head pointing to the right, PU 6 sts in a line down the centre of the back, then work the following rows back and forth (not in the round). Turn your work now, and at the end of each of the following rows. Slip all sts purlwise.

Row 1: Sl1, p5. (6 sts)

Row 2: Sl1, k5.

Row 3: Sl1, p5.

Row 4: Sl1, k3, k2tog. (5 sts)

Row 5: Sl1, p4.

Row 6: Sl1, k4.

Row 7: Sl1, p4.

Row 8: Sl1, k2, k2tog. (4 sts)

Row 9: Sl1, p3.

Row 10: Sl1, k3.

Row 11: Sl1, p3.

Row 12: Sl1, k1, k2tog. (3 sts)

Row 13: Sl1, p2.

Row 14: Sl1, k2.

Row 15: Sl1, p2.

Row 16: Sl1, K2tog. (2 sts)

Row 17: Sl1, p1.

Row 18: K2tog. (1 st)

Cut yarn, thread through last remaining st and pull closed. Weave in loose end on P side of work.

Left wing
Turn your hummingbird around (the head will now be pointing to the left) and PU 6 more sts along the side of the first wing. Work the rounds below, turning your work after each one as you did on the first wing. Slip all sts purlwise.

Row 1: Sl1, p5. (6 sts)

Row 2: Sl1, k5.

Row 3: Sl1, p5.

Row 4: Ssk, k4. (5 sts)

Row 5: Sl1, p4.

Row 6: Sl1, k4.

Row 7: Sl1, p4.

Row 8: Ssk, k3. (4 sts)

Row 9: Sl1, p3.

Row 10: Sl1, k3.

Row 11: Sl1, p3.

Row 12: Ssk, k2. (3 sts)

Row 13: Sl1, p2.

Row 14: Sl1, k2.

Row 15: Sl1, p2.

Row 16: Ssk, k1. (2 sts)

Row 17: Sl1, p1.

Row 18: Ssk. (1 st)

Cut yarn, thread through last remaining st and pull closed. Weave in loose end on P side of work.

Eyes can be embroidered with black yarn, if desired.

If desired, add a strand of yarn to the back of your bird so you can dangle the toy in front of your cat (see page 102).

Mellow mushroom

Skill level: Beginner

These dinky little mushrooms are a fast and fun project. With just a little bit of stuffing and shaping you'll create this instantly recognisable shape. Fill them with catnip and your kitty will love them just as much as you do.

SUPPLIES

- Aran weight yarn in two colours:
  Colour A (stalk and cap): 9 m (10 yards)
  Colour B (underside of cap): 4.5 m (5 yards)
- 3.5 mm double-pointed needles
- Darning needle
- Choice of stuffing (hollowfibre filling or catnip)

Size: 6.5 cm (2½ inches) tall

continued on next page

METHOD

Work begins at bottom of stalk.

With colour A, CO 8 sts onto 3 dpns, leaving a tail of about 20 cm (8 inches). Join in the round and K all sts for about 3.8 cm ($1\frac{1}{2}$ inches) or the desired stalk length. Switch to colour B and work the rounds below:

Round 1: K all sts.

Round 2: [Kfb, k1] 4 times. (12 sts)

Round 3: [Kfb] 12 times. (24 sts)

Rounds 4–7: [K1, p1] 12 times.

Switch back to colour A and work the following rounds:

Round 8: K all sts.

Round 9: P all sts.

Rounds 10–13: K all sts.

Stuff the stalk, adding more stuffing to the bottom half. Continue as follows:

Round 14: [K2tog, k4] 4 times. (20 sts)

Round 15: K all sts.

Round 16: [K2tog, k3] 4 times. (16 sts)

Round 17: K all sts.

Round 18: [K2tog, k2] 4 times. (12 sts)

Round 19: K all sts.

Round 20: [K2tog, k1] 4 times. (8 sts)

Stuff the cap.

Round 21: [K2tog] 4 times. (4 sts)

Cut yarn, thread through remaining live sts and pull closed. Thread yarn onto the darning needle, insert the needle down through the centre of the mushroom cap, and bring out somewhere else in the cap, pulling gently to eliminate the pointy top. Weave in loose ends.

Use CO tail to seam the bottom of the stalk closed.

Critical steps for shaping your mushroom
After seaming the bottom of the stalk closed, insert the tail up through the centre-bottom of the stalk, through the underside and out of the centre-top of the cap. Pull the yarn tail gently in order to draw the stalk upwards and into the underside of the cap. This may cause the stalk to shift to one side, which is fine. Make sure that the top of your mushroom is rounded with no pointy top and the underside of the cap is flattened.

Bumblebee

Bring the great outdoors inside with this great knitted busy busy bumblebee! Dangle him on a long strand of yarn and your cat will love it!

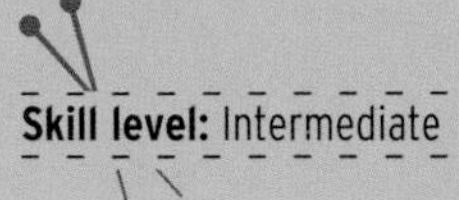

Skill level: Intermediate

METHOD

Work begins at bottom of bee.

With colour A, CO 6 sts onto 3 dpns. Join in the round and work the rounds below.

Note: Do not cut yarn when switching colours, simply carry it on the inside of your work.

Round 1: K all sts.

Round 2: [K1, m1, k1] 3 times. (9 sts)

COLOUR B
Round 3: K all sts.

Round 4: [K1, m1, k2] 3 times. (12 sts)

Round 5: K all sts.

COLOUR A
Round 6: [K1, m1, k3] 3 times. (15 sts)

Round 7: K all sts.

Round 8: [K1, m1, k4] 3 times. (18 sts)

continued on page 32

SUPPLIES

- Aran weight yarn in three colours:
  - **Colour A** (head, body and antennae): 3.6 m (4 yards)
  - **Colour B** (stripes): 2.7 m (3 yards)
  - **Colour C** (wings): 1.8 m (2 yards)
- 3.5 mm double-pointed needles
- Darning needle
- Choice of stuffing (hollowfibre filling or catnip)

Size: 7.5 cm (3 inches) long

COLOUR B
Rounds 9–11: K all sts.

COLOUR A
Round 12: [K2tog, k4] 3 times. (15 sts)

Rounds 13–14: K all sts.

COLOUR B

Round 15: [K2tog, k3] 3 times. (12 sts)

Rounds 16–17: K all sts.

Cut colour B; stuff body firmly. The remainder of the bee is worked in colour A only.

Round 18: [K2tog, k2] 3 times. (9 sts)

Round 19: K all sts.

Round 20: [K1, m1, k1, m1, k1] 3 times. (15 sts)

Rounds 21–23: K all sts.

Round 24: [K2tog, k1, k2tog] 3 times. (9 sts)

Roll a small amount of stuffing into a ball about the size of a grape and insert into the head. There should be no stuffing in your bee's neck. Cut yarn; thread through remaining live sts and pull closed. Secure yarn.

Antennae
Secure two pieces of yarn onto the front of the head, where antennae should go. Make 3–4 knots on top of each other, about 2 cm (¾ inch) from head on both pieces of yarn. Cut each piece just above the knot.

Wings
With colour C, CO 6 sts onto 3 dpns, join in the round and work the rounds below:

Round 1: K all sts.

Round 2: [K1, m1, k1] 3 times. (9 sts)

Rounds 3–6: K all sts.

Round 7: [K2tog, k1] 3 times. (6 sts)

Cut yarn, thread through remaining live sts and pull closed. This is the end that is sewn to your bee's back, just behind the head. Use CO tail to sew the opposite end closed.

If desired, add a strand of yarn to the body of your bee so you can dangle the toy in front of your cat (see page 102).

Desert snake

This slithering serpent is made with a pipe cleaner running through his centre. This means you can easily bend your snake to look like he's wriggling away.

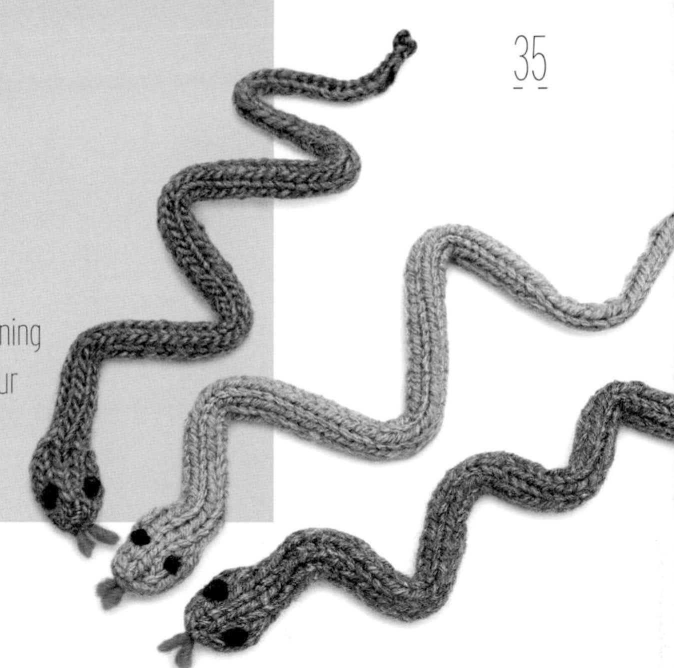

Skill level: Intermediate

METHOD

Work begins at tip of nose.

CO 6 sts onto 3 dpns. Join in the round and work the rounds below:

Rounds 1–2: K all sts.

Round 3: [M1, k2] 3 times. (9 sts)

Rounds 4–6: K all sts.

Round 7: [K2tog, k1] 3 times. (6 sts)

K all sts for 23 cm (9 inches), then insert the pipe cleaner straight into the head and body. The remainder of the snake is worked around it.

Next round: [K2tog] 3 times. (3 sts)

Place all sts on 1 dpn, then work a 3-stitch I-cord (see page 96) for 5 cm (2 inches).

Next round: K2tog, k1. (2 sts)

Work a 2-stitch I-cord for 2.5 cm (1 inch). Cut yarn and thread through last 2 sts. Trim the end of the pipe cleaner if needed. Weave in loose end.

Embroider French knots (see page 101) for the eyes.

With pink yarn, make a loop at the tip of the nose to create the tongue. Cut in the centre.

Bend your snake back and forth to create the illusion of movement.

SUPPLIES

- Aran weight yarn: 9 m (10 yards)
- Scraps of black and pink yarn for eyes and tongue
- 3.5 mm double-pointed needles
- Darning needle
- 30.5-cm (12-inch) pipe cleaner

Size: 30.5 cm (12 inches) long (uncoiled)

Garden snail

There's something so adorable about this little garden snail toy. You'll be amazed at how simple it is to create the shape of the shell – your cat is sure to love it, too.

METHOD

Body
With colour A, CO 4 sts onto 1 dpn. Slip sts to other side of dpn (as with an I-cord). Pull up working yarn from bottom st and K all sts.

Slip sts to other side of dpn again and [m1, k2] twice. Divide 6 sts onto 3 dpns. Join in the round and work the rounds below:

Note: The body can be stuffed a little at a time as you work, or all at once after Round 15. Do not overstuff!

Rounds 1-15: K all sts.

Round 16: K2tog, k4. (5 sts)

Round 17: K all sts.

Round 18: K2tog, k3. (4 sts)

Round 19: K all sts.

Cut yarn, thread through remaining live sts and pull closed. Weave in loose end.

Make two antennae (see page 102) and embroider two small black dots for eyes.

Shell
With colour B, CO 12 sts onto 3 dpns, leaving a tail of about 25 cm (10 inches) for seaming the shell to the body. Join in the round and work the rounds below:

Rounds 1-10: K all sts.

Round 11: K2tog, k10. (11 sts)

Rounds 12-19: K all sts.

Round 20: K2tog, k9. (10 sts)

Rounds 21-26: K all sts.

Round 27: K2tog, k8. (9 sts)

Rounds 28-31: K all sts.

Round 32: K2tog, k7. (8 sts)

Rounds 33-34: K all sts.

Round 35: K2tog, k6. (7 sts)

Rounds 36-37: K all sts.

Round 38: K2tog k5. (6 sts)

Rounds 39-40: K all sts.

Round 41: K2tog, k4. (5 sts)

Rounds 42-43: K all sts.

Round 44: K2tog, k3. (4 sts)

Rounds 45-46: K all sts.

SUPPLIES

- Aran weight yarn in two colours:
  Colour A (body): 4.5 m (5 yards)
  Colour B (shell): 7.3 m (8 yards)
- Scraps of black yarn for eyes
- 3.5 mm double-pointed needles
- Darning needle
- Choice of stuffing (hollowfibre filling or catnip)

Size: 7.5 cm (3 inches) long

Cut yarn, thread through remaining live sts and pull closed. Weave in loose end. Stuff lightly. Seam the open CO edge of the shell to the body about 1.2 cm (½ inch) behind the head. Curl the rest of the shell backwards and around to *one side* of the body. Seam sides of shell together, and to the body.

Twist the shell into a spiral to one side before attaching to the body

Add some details, such as eyes and antennae, using the instructions on pages 100-102

Mr. Grasshopper

This playful critter might seem daunting but this design looks more complex than it really is. With lots of string for your cat to grab and bite, he'll have hours of fun with this minibeast.

METHOD

Work begins at neckline.

CO 9 sts onto 3 dpns. Join in the round and work the rounds below:

Round 1: K all sts.

Round 2: K3, [m1, k1] 3 times, k3. (12 sts)

Rounds 3-17: K all sts.

Round 18: K2tog, k8, ssk. (10 sts)

Rounds 19-22: K all sts.

Round 23: K2tog, k6, ssk. (8 sts)

Rounds 24-27: K all sts.

Round 28: [K2tog] 4 times. (4 sts)

Round 29: K all sts.

Cut yarn, thread through remaining live sts and pull closed. Weave in both loose ends. Stuff body through neck opening. The side of the body with the decreases will be the top of your grasshopper.

Head

CO 6 sts onto 3 dpns. Join in the round and work the rounds below:

Round 1: K all sts.

Round 2: [M1, k2] 3 times. (9 sts)

Rounds 3-4: K all sts.

Round 5: [K2tog, k1] 3 times. (6 sts)

Rounds 6-7: K all sts.

Cut yarn; thread through remaining live sts. Add stuffing, pull closed and seam to neck opening with CO side up. Weave in loose ends.

Note: A portion of the two large legs, and all four of the skinny legs, are created with a single strand of yarn, which is twisted. This is done by holding onto the yarn with one hand, and twisting it with the other hand until it is tight enough to twist around itself when folded in half. One end is then threaded through the grasshopper's body, and a knot is tied near the bottom to keep it from untwisting.

continued on next page

Skill level: Intermediate

SUPPLIES

- Aran weight yarn: 18.25 m (20 yards)
- Scraps of black and yellow yarn for embroidery
- 3.5 mm double-pointed needles
- Darning needle
- Choice of stuffing (hollowfibre filling or catnip)

Size: 11.5 cm (4½ inches) long

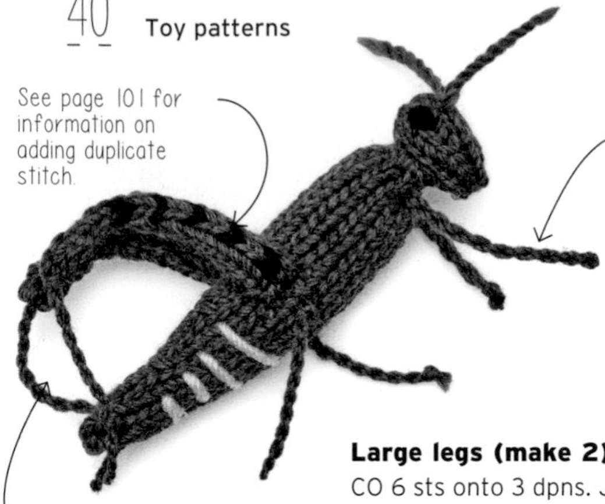

See page 101 for information on adding duplicate stitch.

Attach the front legs just behind Mr. Grasshopper's head.

Twisted 25-cm (10-inch) tail anchors the large legs to the body.

Large legs (make 2)
CO 6 sts onto 3 dpns. Join in the round and work the rounds below:

Rounds 1–3: K all sts.

Round 4: K2tog, k4. (5 sts)

Rounds 5–7: K all sts.

Round 8: K2tog, k3 (all on 1 dpn). (4 sts)

Rows 9–17 of the large legs are worked as an I-cord (see page 96). Sts are slipped to the other side of the dpn after each row, and the working yarn is brought up from the last st:

Rows 9–11: K all sts.

Row 12: K2tog, k2. (3 sts)

Rows 13–15: K all sts.

Row 16: [Kfb] 3 times. (6 sts)

Row 17: K all sts.

Cut yarn, leaving a tail of about 25 cm (10 inches) to make the bottom half of the leg. Thread end through remaining live sts and pull closed.

Twist the 25-cm (10-inch) tail following the instructions on the previous page. Fold so that the twisted portion of the leg is approximately the same length as the knitted portion of the leg (the remainder of the yarn is woven into the knee). If desired, embroider duplicate stitching on the outside of the large part of the leg, as pictured (see page 101).

Seam the CO end to the centre of your grasshopper's body. Please refer to pictures for correct placement of legs.

Thread the bottom of the twisted yarn into a darning needle, and pull through a stitch near the tail end of your grasshopper. Tie a knot close to the end of the twisted yarn to secure in place.

Skinny legs (make 2)
Cut a piece of yarn about 25 cm (10 inches) long. Twist, then fold in half. Thread through your grasshopper just behind the head at the side of the body (refer to pictures for correct leg placement).

Adjust to desired length (about 3.8 cm/1½ inches) on each side of the body. Tie a knot in the end and cut just below the knot.

Prepare a second skinny leg in exactly the same way and thread it through your grasshopper below the large leg.

Embroider the stripes on the tail with yellow yarn and the eyes with black yarn. Add antennae (see page 102 for more information).

Kitten mittens

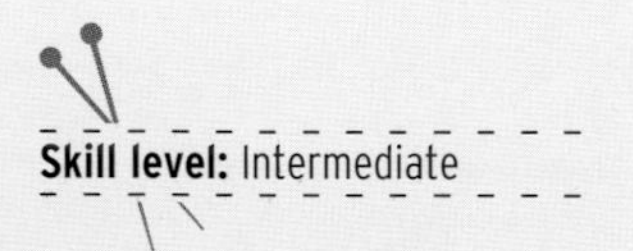

These miniature mittens are real winter warmers and lots of fun for any cat to play with. Work them in a single colour or use any yarn you have to hand to come up with some unique designs.

There's no limit to the designs and embellishments you can add to your mittens.

METHOD

CO 18 sts onto 3 dpns. Join in the round and work the rounds below:

Rounds 1–3: [K1, p1] 9 times.

Rounds 4–5: K all sts.

Round 6: M1, k1, m1, k17. (20 sts)

Round 7: K all sts.

Round 8: M1, k3, m1, k17. (22 sts)

Round 9: Slip first 5 sts onto a piece of scrap yarn, CO 1 new st to the working dpn, k17. (18 sts)

Rounds 10–15: K all sts.

Round 16: [K1, k2tog] 6 times. (12 sts)

Round 17: K all sts.

Cut yarn, thread through remaining live sts and pull closed. Place the 5 live sts on scrap yarn onto 2 dpns.

With a third dpn, PU 3 new sts at inner thumb for a total of 8 sts (see page 96), then K all sts for 3 rounds.

Cut yarn, thread through live sts and pull closed. Weave in loose ends on inside of mitten.

Stuff, then seam closed along bottom. If desired, a second identical mitten can be made and attached to the first with a small piece of yarn.

Mittens can be embellished with stripes as you work, or duplicate stitching (see page 101) afterwards.

SUPPLIES

- Aran weight yarn: 13.75 m (15 yards) for two mittens
- Piece of additional scrap yarn
- 3.5 mm double-pointed needles
- Darning needle
- Choice of stuffing (hollowfibre filling or catnip)

Size: 6.5 cm (2½ inches) long

Jingle-bell ball

Whether he's rolling it across the floor or tossing it up in the air, your cat will love hearing this ball as much as he loves playing with it!

Skill level: Beginner

METHOD

CO 6 sts onto 3 dpns. Join in the round and work the rounds below:

Round 1: K all sts.

Round 2: [M1, k1] 6 times. (12 sts)

Round 3: K all sts.

Round 4: [M1, k2] 6 times. (18 sts)

Round 5: K all sts.

Round 6: [M1, k3] 6 times. (24 sts)

Round 7: K all sts.

Round 8: [M1, k4] 6 times. (30 sts)

Rounds 9–11: K all sts.

Round 12: [K2tog, k3] 6 times. (24 sts)

Round 13: K all sts.

Round 14: [K2tog, k2] 6 times. (18 sts)

Round 15: K all sts.

Round 16: [K2tog, k1] 6 times. (12 sts)

Round 17: K all sts.

Round 18: [K2tog] 6 times. (6 sts)

Round 19: K all sts.

Cut yarn, thread through remaining live sts but do not pull closed yet. Stuff bottom half of ball very firmly. Insert bell; add additional stuffing on all sides and on top of bell. Pull closed; weave in loose ends.

Note: Stripes and patterns can be added in any increments desired.

If desired, add a strand of yarn to your ball so you can dangle the toy in front of your cat (see page 102).

SUPPLIES

- Aran weight yarn: 9 m (10 yards) (in one or more colours)
- 3.5 mm double-pointed needles
- Darning needle
- Choice of stuffing (hollowfibre filling or catnip)
- 1 bell: 2 cm (¾ inch) or smaller

Size: 5 cm (2 inches) diameter

Skill level: Intermediate

Tickle my thistle

Give your cat a hint of Scotland with this charming toy. Luckily there are no sharp points on this thistle, and the top of the flower has a lovely soft texture.

Pattern note: Special stitches

Kfbfbf = Knit into the front, back, front, back and front of one st, creating 4 new sts (a total of 5 sts). This is much easier to do if you keep your working yarn loose.

Kfbf = Knit into the front, back and front of one st, creating 2 new sts (a total of 3 sts).

SUPPLIES

- Aran weight yarn in two colours:
  Colour A (stem and bottom): 4.5 m (5 yards)
  Colour B (flower): 4.5 m (5 yards)
- 3.5 mm double-pointed needles
- Darning needle
- Choice of stuffing (hollowfibre filling or catnip)

Size: 7.5 cm (3 inches) tall (not including stem)

METHOD

Work begins at bottom of stem.

With colour A, CO 3 sts onto 1 dpn, leaving a tail of about 30 cm (12 inches) long (if desired) to dangle the toy in front of your cat, and then work a 3-stitch I-cord (see page 96) for 5 cm (2 inches). Kfbfbf into the first st. Pick up another dpn and repeat in the next stitch. Finally, pick up your last dpn and repeat in the last st. You should now have a total of 15 sts on 3 dpns.

continued on next page

Join in the round and work the rows below:

Round 1: [K1, p1] 7 times, k1.

Round 2: [P1, k1] 7 times, p1.

Round 3: [K1, p1] 7 times, k1.

Round 4: [P1, k1] 7 times, p1.

Round 5: [K1, p1] 7 times, k1.

Round 6: [K2tog, p1, k1, p1] 3 times. (12 sts)

Round 7: [P1, k1] 6 times.

Round 8: [K1, p1] 6 times.

Round 9: [K2tog, p1, k1] 3 times. (9 sts)

Round 10: [P1, k1, p1] 3 times.

Round 11: [K1, p1, k1] 3 times.

Round 12: [K2tog, p1] 3 times. (6 sts)

Round 13: [P1, k1] 3 times.

Round 14: [K1, p1] 3 times.

Stuff the bottom part of the thistle. Cut colour A, join colour B and continue with the following rounds:

Round 15: [Kfbf] 6 times. (18 sts)

Rounds 16–18: K all sts.

Round 19: [K2tog, k1] 6 times. (12 sts)

Round 20: [K2tog] 6 times. (6 sts)

Stuff the flower. Cut yarn, thread through remaining live sts and pull closed. Weave in loose ends.

The top part of the flower is made by adding several strands of yarn, each about 2 cm (¾ inch) long to the top. Separate the plies of yarn and trim to desired length. The more you add, the fluffier your flower will be.

Kitty cat head

Why not re-create your cat in cat-toy form with one of these sweet little kitty heads? See if your cat will recognise herself.

Skill level: Intermediate

SUPPLIES

- Aran weight yarn: 13.75 m (15 yards)
- 3.5 mm double-pointed needles
- Scrap yarn for eyes, whiskers and nose
- Piece of additional scrap yarn
- Darning needle
- Choice of stuffing (hollowfibre filling or catnip)

Size: 7.5 cm (3 inches) wide

METHOD

Work begins at neck opening.

CO 18 sts onto 3 dpns. Join in the round and work the rounds below:

Round 1: K all sts.

Round 2: K1, m1, k7, m1, k2, m1, k7, m1, k1. (22 sts)

Round 3: K all sts.

Round 4: K1, m1, k9, m1, k2, m1, k9, m1, k1. (26 sts)

Round 5: K all sts.

Round 6: K1, m1, k11, m1, k2, m1, k11, m1, k1. (30 sts)

Rounds 7–11: K all sts.

Round 12: K1, ssk, k9, k2tog, k2, ssk, k9, k2tog, k1. (26 sts)

Round 13: K all sts.

Round 14: K1, ssk, k7, k2tog, k2, ssk, k7, k2tog, k1. (22 sts)

Round 15: K all sts.

Ears and top of head

Slip first 4 sts onto 1 dpn without knitting them. Slip next 14 sts onto a piece of scrap yarn. You will now have 8 live sts on 2 dpns: slip 2 or 3 onto a third dpn, join in the round, and work the following rounds:

Round 1: [M1, k4] twice. (10 sts)

Round 2: K all sts.

Round 3: [Ssk, k1, k2tog] twice. (6 sts)

Rounds 4–5: K all sts.

Cut yarn, thread through remaining live sts and pull closed. Weave in loose end.

Slip next 3 sts from the scrap yarn onto 1 dpn. Slip last 3 sts from the scrap yarn on the other side of your cat head onto a second dpn. Hold dpns side by side and join using Kitchener stitch (see page 98).

Place remaining 8 sts onto 3 dpns. Join in the round and, beginning with the next st in line, repeat Rounds 1–5 above and all instructions for the second ear. Use loose ends to darn holes on the inside of the ears closed.

Stuff the cat head from the neck opening. Stuffing can be moved inside the ears (if desired) with a dpn from the outside.

Embroider eyes, nose and whiskers.

Seam neck opening closed.

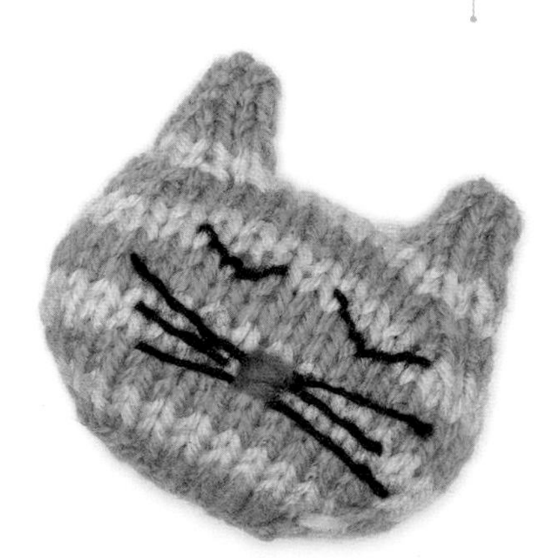

Butterfly kisses

Skill level: Advanced

This delicate butterfly is another fantastic toy for cats who love to leap around. The realistic fluttering is sure to attract and enchant any curious cat.

Spots can be embroidered onto wings with colour C.

Antennae can be added by threading a small piece of colour A yarn through the top of the body and knotting it.

METHOD

Body

With colour A, CO 3 sts onto 1 dpn and knit a 3-stitch I-cord (see page 96) for 5 cm (2 inches). Cut yarn and weave in both loose ends.

Wings

Beginning at one end of the I-cord body, PU 10 sts along one side (see page 96), turn work and, with colour B, K the following rows back and forth, turning work after each row.

Note: Most of the rows begin with a slipped stitch. These should all be slipped purlwise with yarn held at the back of work.

Rows 1–5: Sl1, k9. (10 sts)

Rows 6–9: Sl1, k5. (6 sts)

Row 10: Ssk, k2, k2tog. (4 sts)

Row 11: Sl1, k3.

Row 12: Ssk, k2tog. (2 sts)

Row 13: Sl1, k1.

Cut yarn, thread through remaining live sts and weave in loose ends.

With RS facing you, join colour B again and work the following rows:

Rows 1–4: Sl1, k3. (4 sts)

Row 5: Ssk, k2tog. (2 sts)

Row 6: Sl1, k1.

Cut yarn, thread through remaining live sts and weave in loose ends.

With RS facing you, PU 10 sts along opposite side of body, turn work and, with colour B, knit the following rows back and forth, turning work after each row:

Rows 1–5: Sl1, k9. (10 sts)

Rows 6–9: Sl1, k3. (4 sts)

Row 10: Ssk, k2tog. (2 sts)

Row 11: Sl1, k1.

Cut yarn, thread through remaining 2 sts and weave in loose ends.

With RS facing you, join colour B again and work the following rows:

Rows 1–4: Sl1, k5. (6 sts)

Row 5: Ssk, k2, k2tog. (4 sts)

Row 6: Sl1, k3.

Row 7: Ssk, k2tog. (2 sts)

Row 8: Sl1, k1.

Cut yarn, thread through remaining live sts and weave in loose ends.

If desired, add a strand of yarn to the back of your butterfly so you can dangle the toy in front of your cat (see page 102).

SUPPLIES

- Aran weight yarn in three colours:
  - **Colour A** (body and antennae): 2.75 m (3 yards)
  - **Colour B** (wings): 5.5 m (6 yards)
  - **Colour C** (spots): 1 m (1 yard)
- Two 3.5 mm double-pointed needles
- Darning needle

Size: 5 x 7.5 cm (2 x 3 inches)

Happy birthday Bella!

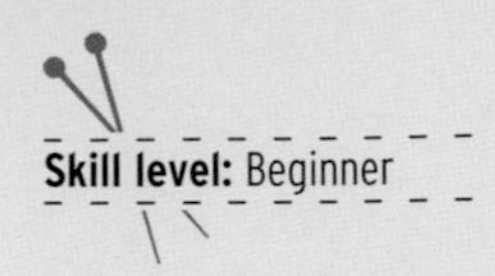
Skill level: Beginner

Bella just loves her beautiful birthday cake. A little catnip treat inside will have your cat feeling like all her birthdays have come at once!

METHOD

Petit-four
Work begins at centre-top.

CO 8 sts onto 3 or 4 dpns. You may find it easier to cast onto 4 dpns so you can easily visualise the square shape, although casting onto 3 dpns will work just fine. Join in the round and work the rounds below:

Round 1: K all sts.

Round 2: [M1, k1] 8 times. (16 sts)

Round 3: K all sts.

Round 4: [M1, k2] 8 times. (24 sts)

Round 5: K all sts.

Round 6: [M1p, k6] 4 times. (28 sts)

Round 7: K all sts.

Round 8: [P1, k6] 4 times.

Round 9: K all sts.

Round 10: [P1, k6] 4 times.

Round 11: K all sts.

Round 12: [P1, k6] 4 times.

Round 13: K all sts.

Round 14: [P1, k6] 4 times.

Round 15: K all sts.

Cast off all sts. Cut yarn, leaving a tail of about 30 cm (12 inches) for seaming.

continued on page 59

SUPPLIES

- Aran weight yarn: 13.75 m (15 yards)
- Scrap yarn in two additional colours for leaf and rosebud
- 3.5 mm double-pointed needles
- Darning needle
- Choice of stuffing (hollowfibre filling or catnip)

Size: 5 cm (2 inches) tall

Bottom square (work flat with 2 dpns)
CO 9 sts onto 1 dpn, then work the rows below. All slip sts should be slipped purlwise.

Row 1: Sl1, p8.

Row 2: Sl1, k8.

Row 3: Sl1, p8.

Row 4: Sl1, k8.

Row 5: Sl1, p8.

Row 6: Sl1, k8.

Row 7: Sl1, p8.

Row 8: Sl1, k8.

Row 9: Sl1, p8.

Row 10: Sl1, k8.

Cast off all sts and weave in loose ends on the P side of the work. Seam 3 sides of this square to the bottom of your petit-four with the P side of the work on the inside. Be sure to line up the corners of the bottom square with the columns of P sts on the petit-four. Stuff, then close seam. Use the CO tail to seam the hole in the top closed. Weave in loose ends.

Leaf (work flat with 2 dpns)
CO 2 sts onto 1 dpn and work the rows below:

Row 1: P all sts.

Row 2: [M1, k1] twice. (4 sts)

Row 3: P all sts.

Row 4: K all sts.

Row 5: [P2tog] twice. (2 sts)

Row 6: K2tog. (1 st)

Cut yarn and thread through remaining st. Weave in loose end on P side. Using the CO tail, seam leaf to centre of your petit four.

Rosebud (work flat with 2 dpns)
CO 5 sts onto 1 dpn and work the rows below:

Row 1: P all sts.

Row 2: K3, k2tog. (4 sts)

Row 3: P all sts.

Row 4: K2, k2tog. (3 sts)

Row 5: P all sts.

Row 6: K1, k2tog. (2 sts)

Row 7: P all sts.

Row 8: K2tog. (1 st)

Cut yarn and thread through remaining st. Weave in loose end on P side. Beginning at CO edge, roll work towards opposite (small) end. Using the CO tail, stitch together at the bottom, then seam to the centre of the petit-four.

Fish out of water

Skill level: Intermediate

Your cat doesn't need to go anywhere near water to play with this fish! She'll love the colourful tail fins which hang down through the centre.

SUPPLIES

- Aran weight yarn:
  Colour A: 4.5 m (5 yards)
  Various other colours: 3.6 m (4 yards) in total
- 3.5 mm double-pointed needles
- Darning needle
- Choice of stuffing (hollowfibre filling or catnip)

Size: 6.5 cm (2½ inches) long (not including tail)

Fill with irresistible catnip

METHOD

Work begins at mouth.

With colour A, CO 6 sts onto 3 dpns. Join in the round and work the rounds below:

Round 1: K all sts.

Round 2: [M1, k2, m1, k1] twice. (10 sts)

Rounds 3–4: K all sts.

Round 5: [M1, k4, m1, k1] twice. (14 sts)

Cut colour A, leaving a 20-cm (8-inch) tail.

Rounds 6–13: All sts for the next 8 rounds are knitted. Stripes of different colours are added in this section. The number of rounds for each colour is optional, as long as 8 rounds in total are worked. For example, use 2 different colours (4 rounds each), 4 different colours (2 rounds each) or 8 different colours (1 round each), etc. Leave a 20-cm (8-inch) tail when joining each new colour, and another 20-cm (8-inch) tail when cutting yarn.

continued on page 63

After the 8 striped rounds, add stuffing to the body of your fish, keeping in mind that fish are more flat than round. The next section is worked in colour A again and around the multi-coloured tail fins (pieces of yarn) which will hang down through the centre of your work.

Round 14: K1, ssk, k2tog, k3, ssk, k2tog, k2. (10 sts)

Rounds 15–17: K all sts.

Round 18: [Ssk, k2tog, k1] twice. (6 sts)

Rounds 19–21: K all sts.

Cut yarn leaving a 20-cm (8-inch) tail; thread through remaining live sts. Pull tightly closed around all of the tail fins (pieces of yarn); secure. Weave in tail from the CO sts.

Trim tail fins to desired length, approximately 10 cm (4 inches) long.

If desired, add a strand of yarn to the head of your fish so you can dangle the toy in front of your cat (see page 102).

Tip In order to anchor the new colour to your work and to minimise jogging of stripes, work the first stitch of each new colour together with the previous colour (wrap both colours around your needle). On the next round, knit both colours together for your first stitch.

Leaping lizard

Transport your feline friend to the savannah with this wonderful lizard. He'll love carrying his new toy around by the handy tail.

Skill level: Advanced

METHOD

Work begins at tip of nose.

CO 3 sts onto 1 dpn. Slip the sts to the other side of your needle (as in an I-cord), and K all 3 sts. Then slip the sts to the other side of the needle again and work [m1, k1] 3 times. Divide the 6 sts onto 3 dpns and join in the round. Work the rounds below:

Rounds 1-2: K all sts. (6 sts)

Round 3: [M1, k2] 3 times. (9 sts)

Rounds 4-6: K all sts.

Round 7: [K2tog, k1] 3 times. (6 sts)

Round 8: K all sts.

Round 9: [M1, k2] 3 times. (9 sts)

Rounds 10-11: K all sts.

Round 12: [M1, k3] 3 times. (12 sts)

Rounds 13-20: K all sts.

Round 21: [K2tog, k2] 3 times. (9 sts)

Rounds 22-25: K all sts.

Stuff your lizard with a small amount of stuffing at this point, keeping in mind that lizards are more flat than round. Continue with the rounds below:

Tip: Stuffing can be shifted around and moved into the head and tail by using a dpn and working on the outside of the body.

Round 26: [K2tog, k1] 3 times. (6 sts)

Rounds 27-32: K all sts.

Round 33: [K2tog] 3 times (work all of these on one dpn). (3 sts)

Work 6 rows of a 3-stitch I-cord (see page 96).

Next row: K2tog, k1.

Then work 10 rows of a 2-stitch I-cord.

Cut yarn and weave in loose ends.

continued on page 67

SUPPLIES

- Aran weight yarn: 13.7 m (15 yards)
- Scraps of black yarn for eyes
- 3.5 mm double-pointed needles
- Darning needle
- Choice of stuffing (hollowfibre filling or catnip)

Size: 15 cm (6 inches) long

Front legs (make 2)
Determine which side you want to be the top of your lizard. Both sides are basically the same, but one side may look a little better to you.

While looking down at the top, PU 3 sts (see page 96) along one edge, just behind the head. Work 3 rows of a 3-stitch I-cord (see page 96). Cut yarn and weave in loose ends on the bottom of your lizard.

Back legs (make 2)
While looking down at the top, PU 3 sts along one edge, just behind the belly. Work 5 rows of a 3-stitch I-cord.

Cut yarn and weave in loose ends on the bottom of your lizard.

Eyes
Embroider eyes with black yarn (see page 101).

Along came a spider

Spiders might not be everybody's favourite creatures, but there's nothing to be squeamish about with this incy wincy knitted spider.

Skill level: Beginner

METHOD

Work begins at tip of head.

CO 6 sts onto 3 dpns. Join in the round and work the rounds below:

Round 1: K all sts.

Round 2: [M1, k1] 6 times. (12 sts)

Rounds 3–5: K all sts.

Round 6: [K2tog] 6 times. (6 sts)

Round 7: [M1, k1] 6 times. (12 sts)

Round 8: K all sts.

Round 9: [M1, k2] 6 times. (18 sts)

Rounds 10–17: K all sts.

Round 18: [K2tog, k1] 6 times. (12 sts)

Round 19: K all sts.

Cut yarn; thread through remaining live sts. Stuff head and body firmly. Pull closed and secure yarn. Weave in both loose ends.

Legs

Legs are made with pieces of the same yarn. Thread a darning needle with yarn, insert into side of head, pulling needle through on the opposite side of head until 5 cm (2 inches) remain. Take one small stitch to secure yarn, then cut at 5 cm (2 inches) from head (both legs should be the same length).

Repeat 3 more times, each leg slightly behind the other, for a total of 8 legs.

If desired, add a strand of yarn to the back of your spider so you can dangle the toy in front of your cat (see page 102).

SUPPLIES

- Aran weight yarn: 9 m (10 yards)
- 3.5 mm double-pointed needles
- Darning needle
- Choice of stuffing (hollowfibre filling or catnip)

Size: 6.5 cm (2½ inches) long

Green frog of happiness

This little froggy will make you smile – and kitty will love it, too. The finished toy looks more complex than it is so don't be discouraged.

Skill level: Intermediate

METHOD

Work begins at tip of nose.

CO 6 sts onto 3 dpns. Join in the round and work the rounds below:

Round 1: K all sts.

Round 2: [M1, k2] 3 times. (9 sts)

Round 3: K all sts.

Round 4: [M1, k3] 3 times. (12 sts)

Round 5: K all sts.

Round 6: K1, MB, k2, MB, k7.

Rounds 7-8: K all sts.

Round 9: K1, m1, k4, m1, k2, m1, k4, m1, k1. (16 sts)

Round 10: K all sts.

Round 11: K1, m1, k6, m1, k2, m1, k6, m1, k1. (20 sts)

Rounds 12-14: K all sts.

Round 15: K1, ssk, k4, k2tog, k2, ssk, k4, k2tog, k1. (16 sts)

Rounds 16-17: K all sts.

Round 18: K1, ssk, k2, k2tog, k2, ssk, k2, k2tog, k1. (12 sts)

Rounds 19-20: K all sts.

Round 21: K1, ssk, k2tog, k2, ssk, k2tog, k1. (8 sts)

Rounds 22-23: K all sts.

Stuff head and body. The remaining 8 sts will be used to make the back legs.

continued on page 72

Pattern note: Special stitches
MB = Make a bobble (for the eyes).

To work this stitch:

Kfbf, turn
P3, turn
K3, turn
P3, turn
Sl2 purlwise, k1
Pass 2 sl sts over knitted st
and off needle

SUPPLIES

- Aran weight yarn: 13.75 m (15 yards)
- Scraps of black yarn (for eyes, optional)
- Piece of additional scrap yarn
- 3.5 mm double-pointed needles
- Darning needle
- Choice of stuffing (hollowfibre filling or catnip)

Size: 5 cm (2 inches) tall

Back legs

Round 1: M1, k2, slip next 4 sts onto a piece of scrap yarn, join first 3 sts in round with last 2 sts, m1, k2. (6 sts)

Rounds 2–9: K all sts.

Round 10: K2tog, k4. (5 sts)

Rounds 11–18: K all sts.

Round 19: K2tog, k3 all on 1 dpn. (4 sts)

Slip sts to the other side of dpn, work 8 rows of a 4-stitch I-cord (see page 96), then turn work instead of slipping sts to other side of dpn (the working yarn is now coming from the top st). Work the following rows back and forth (not in the round) to shape the foot:

Row 1: P all sts.

Row 2: K all sts.

Row 3: P all sts.

Row 4: Ssk, k2tog. (2 sts)

Row 5: P2tog. (1 st)

Cut yarn and thread through remaining st. Weave in loose end on P side of work.

Place 4 sts from the scrap yarn onto 2 dpns. Rejoin yarn at first st on scrap yarn then work [m1, k2] twice. Spread the sts over 3 dpns and join in the round. Work Rounds 2–19 above for the second leg and then Rows 1–5 to shape the second foot.

Add additional stuffing, if required, through the hole between the legs, then seam the hole closed. Fold legs as pictured and seam in place.

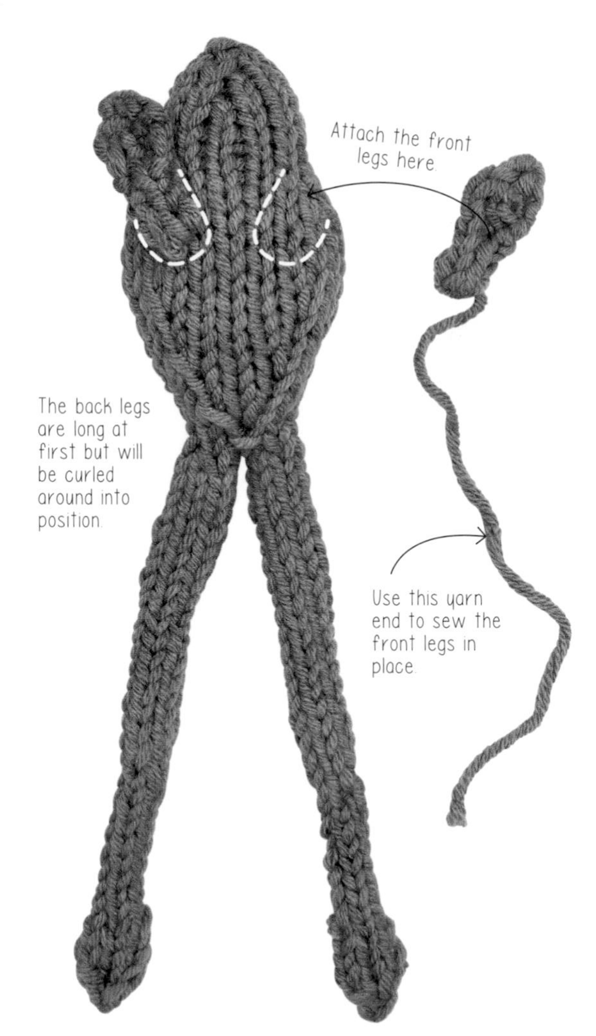

Front legs (make 2)

CO 4 sts onto 1 dpn.

Slip sts to the other side of dpn, and work 4 rows of a 4-stitch I-cord.

For the foot, work Rows 1–5 of the foot section of Back Legs (page 72).

Seam to bottom of frog, as pictured.

With the black yarn, embroider detail onto the eyes, if desired (see page 101).

Your frog will look like this from underneath.

Fold the back legs in this shape before seaming them to the body.

Shrimpy

Skill level: Advanced

Shrimpy is a fun, quirky design for those who want to try something a little different. Your cat might well prefer a real shrimp but this will keep him happy.

METHOD

Work begins at tip of nose.

CO 3 sts onto 1 dpn.

Slip sts to the other side of dpn, and work two rows of a 3-stitch I-cord (see page 96).

Slip sts to the other side of dpn one more time, then work [m1, k1] 3 times.

Divide the 6 sts onto 3 dpns. Join in the round and work the following rounds:

Rounds 1-2: K all sts.

Round 3: M1, k5, m1, k1. (8 sts)

Rounds 4-5: K all sts.

Round 6: M1, k7, m1, k1. (10 sts)

Rounds 7-11: K all sts.

Round 12: P all sts.

Rounds 13-17: K all sts.

Round 18: P all sts.

The short rows below will create the curve in your shrimp's back (see page 97 for instructions on working short rows). Each one is worked exactly the same and will begin and end at the start of the round.

Round 19: K7, wt, p4, wt, k7.

Round 20: K all sts.

Round 21: K7, wt, p4, wt, k7.

Round 22: P all sts.

Round 23: K7, wt, p4, wt, k7.

Round 24: K all sts.

Round 25: K7, wt, p4, wt, k7.

Round 26: P all sts.

Round 27: K7, wt, p4, wt, k7.

Round 28: K all sts.

Round 29: K7, wt, p4, wt, k7.

Round 30: P all sts.

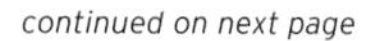

continued on next page

SUPPLIES

- Aran weight yarn: 18.25 m (20 yards)
- Scraps of black yarn for eyes
- 3.5 mm double-pointed needles
- Darning needle
- Choice of stuffing (hollowfibre filling or catnip)

Size: 18 cm (7 inches) long when uncurled

Rounds 31–32: K all sts.

Round 33: K2tog, k6, ssk. (8 sts)

Rounds 34–37: K all sts.

Round 38: P all sts.

Round 39: K all sts.

Round 40: [M1, k2] 4 times. (12 sts)

Rounds 41–45: K all sts.

Add a small amount of stuffing at this point, excluding the last 7 rounds (the tail) which will remain unstuffed and be flattened. Stuffing can be distributed inside of your shrimp by using a dpn from the outside. Be careful not to overstuff!

Round 46: K1, ssk, k2tog, k2, ssk, k2tog, k1. (8 sts)

Round 47: K all sts.

Cut yarn, thread through remaining live sts and pull closed. Weave in loose end.

With black yarn, make French knots for the eyes (see page 101).

Add two long antennae (about 7.5 cm/3 inches) and eight long legs (four on each side, about 2.5 cm/1 inch) to the head, and ten short legs (five on each side, about 1.3 cm/½ inch) to the middle of the body (see page 102).

The tail remains flat — don't add any stuffing here.

French knots make fantastic eyes.

Dragonfly drop

This is a great toy for energetic, playful cats that love to leap around. Use a strand of yarn to make the dragonfly jump and fly, and excite and delight your kitty.

METHOD

Body
Work begins at tip of tail.

With the aran weight yarn, CO 3 sts onto 1 dpn.

Slip sts to the other side of dpn, and work a 3-stitch I-cord for 5 cm (2 inches) (see page 96).

Kfb in the first st with a dpn, kfb in the next st with a second dpn and kfb in the last st with a third dpn.

Join in the round and work the following rounds:

Rounds 1-5: K all sts. (6 sts)

Round 6: [K2tog] 3 times. (3 sts)

Round 7: [Kfb] 3 times. (6 sts)

Round 8: K all sts.

Round 9: [Kfb, k1] 3 times. (9 sts)

Cut yarn, thread through remaining live sts and pull closed. Weave in loose ends.

Wings (make 4)
With the 4 ply yarn, CO 6 sts onto 3 dpns. Join in the round and work the rounds below:

Rounds 1-2: K all sts.

Round 3: M1, k6. (7 sts)

Attach the wings with curved edges facing downwards and away from the head so they spread out like real wings.

Rounds 4-5: K all sts.

Round 6: M1, k7. (8 sts)

Rounds 7-8: K all sts.

Round 9: M1, k8. (9 sts)

Rounds 10-11: K all sts.

Round 12: K2tog, k7. (8 sts)

Rounds 13-14: K all sts.

Round 15: K2tog, k6. (7 sts)

Rounds 16-17: K all sts.

Cut yarn, thread through remaining live sts and pull closed. Weave in all loose ends. Flatten all wings and seam them to the body as pictured above, with curved edges facing downwards (away from the head).

With the black yarn, make 2 antennae and embroider two small dots for eyes.

If desired, add a strand of yarn to the head of your dragonfly so your toy can 'fly' (see page 102).

SUPPLIES

- Aran weight yarn: 4.5 m (5 yards)
- 4 ply yarn: 9 m (10 yards)
- Scraps of black yarn (for eyes and antennae)
- 3.5 mm double-pointed needles
- Darning needle

Size: 11.5 cm (4½ inches) long

See pages 101-102 for more information about adding antennae and eyes.

Seam the wings to the body carefully so your dragonfly can withstand playtime!

- Aran weight yarn in two colours:

  Colour A (head, belly, legs and spots): 4.5 m (5 yards)

  Colour B (wings): 4.5 m (5 yards)
- 3.5 mm double-pointed needles
- Darning needle
- Choice of stuffing (hollowfibre filling or catnip)

Size: 6.5 cm (2½ inches) long

Work begins at tip of head.

With colour A, CO 6 sts onto 3 dpns. Join in the round and work the rounds below:

Round 1: K all sts.

Round 2: [M1, k2] 3 times. (9 sts)

Round 3: K all sts.

The remainder of your ladybird is worked back and forth (not in the round) on 2 dpns. Turn work, sl1 purlwise, then p5 all on 1 dpn. This will be the new beginning/end of row. (3 live sts will remain on another dpn for working later.) Cut colour A, join colour B and work the rows below. All slip sts should be slipped purlwise.

Row 1: K all sts. (6 sts)

Row 2: P all sts.

Row 3: Sl1, [m1, k1] 5 times. (11 sts)

Row 4: Sl1, p10.

Row 5: Sl1, [m1, k2] 5 times. (16 sts)

Row 6: Sl1, p15.

Row 7: Sl1, k15.

Row 8: Sl1, p15.

Row 9: Sl1, k15.

Row 10: Sl1, p15.

Row 11: Sl1, k5, ssk, k2tog, k6. (14 sts)

Row 12: Sl1, p13.

Row 13: Sl1, k4, ssk, k2tog, k5. (12 sts)

Row 14: Sl1, p11.

Row 15: Sl1, k3, ssk, k2tog, k4. (10 sts)

Row 16: Sl1, p9.

Row 17: Sl1, k2, ssk, k2tog, k3. (8 sts)

Row 18: Sl1, p7.

Cut colour B, rejoin colour A, leaving a tail of 20–25 cm (8–10 inches) to seam wings to bottom afterwards. Continue with the rows below:

Row 19: K all sts.

Row 20: Sl1, p7.

Row 21: Sl1, k7.

Row 22: Sl1, p7.

Row 23: Sl1, k7.

Row 24: Sl1, p7.

Row 25: Sl1, k7.

Row 26: Sl1, p7.

Row 27: Sl1, k7.

Row 28: Sl1, p7.

Row 29: Sl1, k7.

Row 30: Sl1, p7.

Row 31: Ssk, k4, k2tog. (6 sts)

Row 32: Sl1, p5.

Row 33: Ssk, k2, k2tog. (4 sts)

Row 34: Sl1, p3.

Row 35: Sl1, k2tog, k1. (3 sts)

Row 36: Sl1, p2.

Row 37: Sl1, k2.

Row 38: Sl1, p2.

continued on page 85

Miss Ladybird

Skill level: Beginner

Little Miss Ladybird is a pet favourite and lots of fun. Stuff her firmly with hollowfibre filling or catnip for a robust toy that your furball won't want to put down.

Fold the bottom of your ladybird underneath the wings. Cut yarn and thread through the 3 live head sts first, then through the 3 live body sts. Pull closed and weave in all loose ends on P side of work.

Seam the top of the ladybird (wings) to the bottom on all sides, stuffing firmly just before closing.

With colour A, add antennae to the head and 6 legs (3 on each side) to the body (see page 102).

With colour A, embroider spots with satin stitch (see page 101).

Raccoon tail

This is a nice, big toy that can withstand a lot of pouncing, clawing and biting, so it is fantastic for cats who really like to play hard!

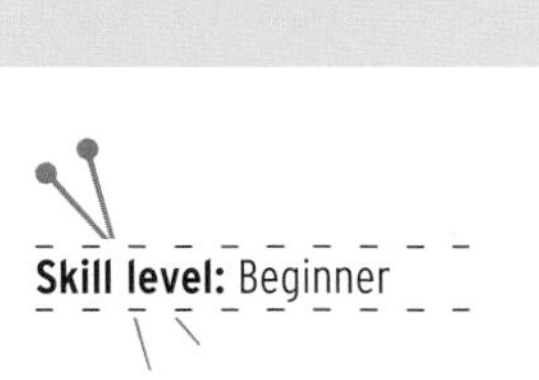

Skill level: Beginner

SUPPLIES

- Aran weight yarn in two contrasting colours:
  - **Colour A** (darker colour): 7.25 m (8 yards)
  - **Colour B** (lighter colour): 9 m (10 yards)
- 3.5 mm double-pointed needles
- Darning needle
- Choice of stuffing (hollowfibre filling or catnip)

Size: 15 cm (6 inches) long

METHOD

Work begins at larger end.

With colour A, CO 18 sts onto 3 dpns, leaving a tail of about 20 cm (8 inches). If you'd like to dangle the toy in front of your cat, leave a longer tail, about 30-38 cm (12-15 inches). Join in the round and work the rounds below:

Round 1 (colour A): K all sts.

Rounds 2-4 (colour B): K all sts.

Rounds 5-6 (colour A): K all sts.

Tip To achieve the best finish and minimise jogging of stripes, simply bring the new yarn over the old one when changing colours.

Repeat the pattern of Rounds 2-6 (working 3 rounds of colour B followed by 2 rounds of colour A) five more times, until there are a total of seven colour A stripes. Then work the following rounds:

Round 1 (colour B): K all sts.

Round 2 (colour B): [K4, k2tog] 3 times. (15 sts)

Round 3 (colour B): K all sts.

Round 4 (colour A): K all sts.

Round 5 (colour A): [K3, k2tog] 3 times. (12 sts)

Round 6 (colour A): K all sts.

Round 7 (colour A): [K2, k2tog] 3 times. (9 sts)

Round 8 (colour A): K all sts.

Cut yarn, thread through remaining live sts and pull closed. Weave in loose end.

Stuff tail lightly, then use the CO tail to seam closed the open end. If desired, thread the yarn tail through the centre of the closed end and leave dangling.

Lazy daisy

Who could resist this pretty floral design? Use whatever colourful yarn you have to create your own beautiful flower. Why not try a different colour for each petal?

METHOD

Stem

With colour A, CO 3 sts onto 1 dpn, and work a 3-stitch I-cord (see page 96) for 10 cm (4 inches).

Next row: [Kfb] 3 times. (6 sts)

Divide sts onto 3 dpns (2 sts on each). Join in the round and work the rounds below:

Round 1: K all sts.

Round 2: [Kfb] 6 times. (12 sts)

Centre of daisy

Cut colour A. Join colour B and work the rounds below:

Rounds 1–3: K all sts.

Round 4: [K2tog] 6 times. (6 sts)

Round 5: [K2tog] 3 times. (3 sts)

Cut colour B, thread through remaining live sts, tucking in loose ends and pull tightly closed. Insert darning needle down into centre and pull through, flattening out the centre of the daisy. Weave in loose end.

Petals

Stitches are now picked up in the last round of colour A sts to work the petals (see page 96). With colour C yarn and centre of daisy facing you, PU each side of one of the sts in the last round of colour A (it doesn't matter where you begin). Turn work, and work the following rows back and forth (not in the round):

Row 1: Sl1 purlwise, m1p, p1. (3 sts)

Row 2: Sl1 purlwise, k2.

Row 3: Sl1 purlwise, m1p, p2. (4 sts)

Row 4: Sl1 purlwise, k3.

Row 5: Sl1 purlwise, p3.

Repeat Rows 4–5 four more times for a total of 10 rows in stocking stitch, then work the following row:

Next row: Ssk, k2tog. (2 sts)

Cut yarn, thread through remaining sts, pull closed and weave in loose end on P side of work. Use the PU tail to reinforce the spot where the picked-up sts meet the centre of the daisy.

Repeat five more times, arranging the petals around the daisy for a total of six petals.

SUPPLIES

- Aran weight yarn in three colours:
  - **Colour A** (stem): 3.6 m (4 yards)
  - **Colour B** (centre): 2.7 m (3 yards)
  - **Colour C** (petals): 9 m (10 yards)
- 3.5 mm double-pointed needles
- Darning needle

Size: 7.5 x 12.5 cm (3 x 5 inches)

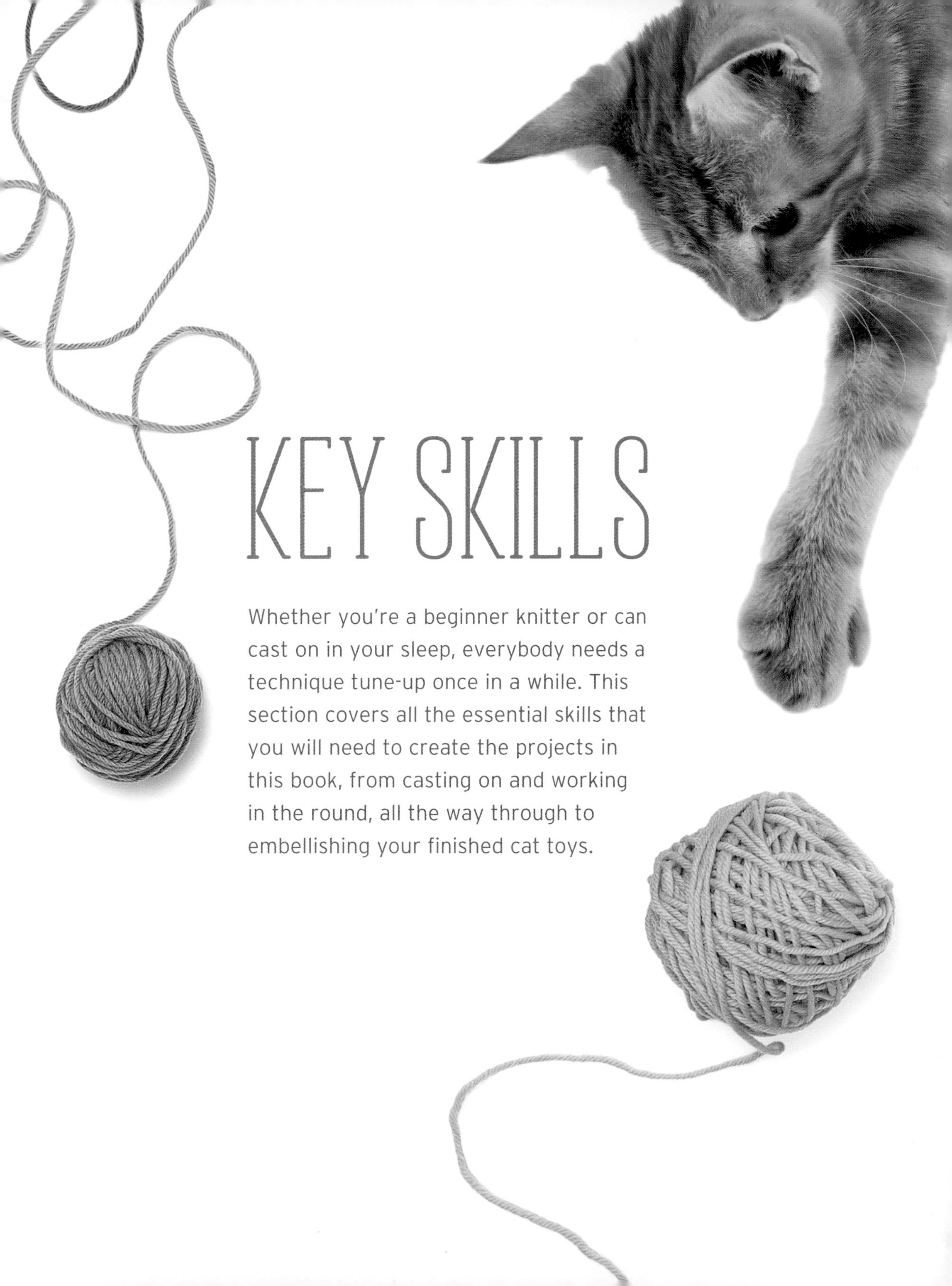

KEY SKILLS

Whether you're a beginner knitter or can cast on in your sleep, everybody needs a technique tune-up once in a while. This section covers all the essential skills that you will need to create the projects in this book, from casting on and working in the round, all the way through to embellishing your finished cat toys.

Materials and equipment

Knitting cat toys has never been simpler or more fun. They're a great way to use up scraps of yarn that you might have left over from other projects, and no special tools are required. So grab some needles, open up your stash drawer and tell Kitty to get ready for some fun!

Yarns

Yarns are available in a range of weights, from 1 ply to extra chunky. Because yarns may vary from one manufacturer to another and certainly change from one fibre to another, only generic yarn types are indicated for the toys in this book. Each project lists the suggested yarn weight to use. You can choose whatever colours you like, but we have made suggestions in some places.

The yarn weight and needle sizes suggested will help you end up with a cat toy about the listed size (depending on your knitting style and tension). But you could make any of the toys out of the yarn weight of your choice, just make sure to go down at least two needle sizes from what is recommended on the ball band. This is necessary in order to create a tighter-than-average fabric through which stuffing will not show, or, if catnip is used in place of stuffing, it does not fall out.

It's often a good idea to separate your yarns into colour groups and keep these in transparent plastic containers so that you have a palette of colours to work with.

Knitting needles

The needle size used for each of the projects in this book is detailed alongside the pattern. Each of the projects uses double-pointed needles (often referred to as dpns). These are different from conventional needles as they have points on both ends, which allows you to work in the round. They come in sets of 4 or 5, and in the same sizes as conventional needles. Most of these patterns are worked in the round on four dpns. There are a few components which are worked flat with only two dpns.

EQUIVALENT NEEDLE SIZES

Choosing the correct size of needle is crucial to obtaining a good fabric, so try to build up a collection so that you can easily substitute one size for another. Needles are sized in Europe from 2 mm to 15 mm and in the US from 0 to about 19. There is not always an exact match between the two systems.

Europe	US
2 mm	0
2.25 mm	1
2.75 mm	2
3 mm	3
3.25 mm	4
3.5 mm	5
4 mm	6
4.5 mm	7
5 mm	8
5.5 mm	9
6 mm	10
6.5 or 7 mm	10.5
8 mm	11
9 mm	13
10 mm	15
12 or 13 mm	17
15 mm	19

Tape measure
For measuring the length of your work, which is required in some of the patterns.

Row counters
A row counter may help you keep track of the number of rows you have worked. These patterns indicate any change to stitch-count at the end of all applicable rounds by including the new number of stitches. This is very helpful in keeping track of where you are.

Scissors
It's always handy to have a nice small pair of sharp scissors during a knitting project. You'll need them for snipping off yarn ends and surplus threads.

Darning needle
For the patterns in this book, a darning needle is used primarily to draw your working yarn through the remaining stitches at the end of the piece or weave in loose ends. They may also, in rare instances, be used for seaming. They are blunt-tipped with a large eye and available in several sizes to suit different yarn types. They are sometimes called tapestry needles and are designed to not split the yarn.

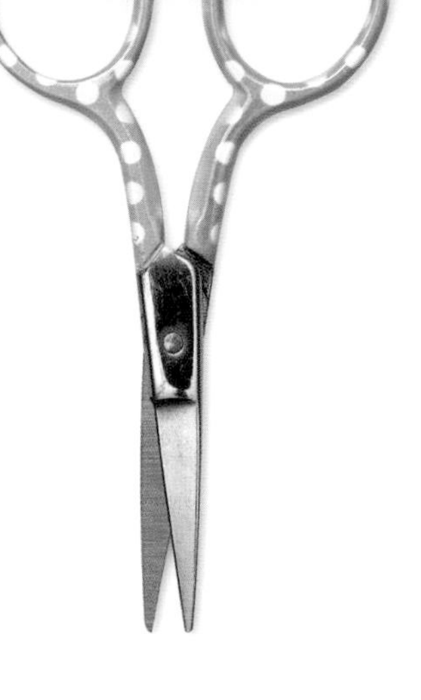

Stuffing materials
There are a number of options when it comes to stuffing your cat toys, including foam or cotton batting, but I recommend either polyester hollowfibre filling or catnip. You can even cut up bits of yarn to use, since most of these toys are so small.

Polyester hollowfibre filling
This is a synthetic, washable fibre that is extremely lightweight. It has a soft feel and it bounces back into shape. It tends to clump less than many of the other stuffing materials. It is also widely available.

Catnip
This is the common name for *Nepeta cataria*, a plant in the mint family. It is native to parts of Europe and Asia and has been widely naturalised in North America, and many cats absolutely go nuts for it! Not all cats are susceptible to the allure of the plant, and reactions vary from cat to cat - some becoming super playful, others blissfully calm. But if your cat is a catnip fan, he/she will be over the moon to find his/her new favourite toy is stuffed with it. The effects of catnip aren't limited to your little kitty either - even lions and tigers can't get enough!

Hollowfibre filling

Catnip

Core techniques

Here you'll find all the techniques that you'll need to be familiar with to complete the patterns in this book. A refresher on the basic knitting stitches can be found on pages 103–105.

Slipknot

1 Putting a slipknot on the needle makes the first stitch of the cast on. Loop the yarn around two fingers of the left hand, the ball end on top. Dip the needle into the loop, catch the ball end of the yarn and pull it through the loop.

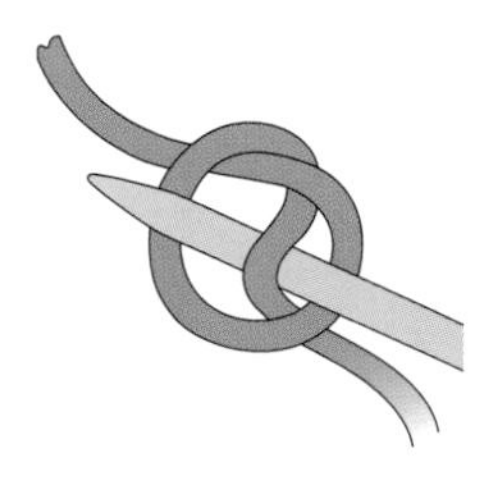

2 Pull the ends of the yarn to tighten the knot. Tighten the ball end to bring the knot up to the needle.

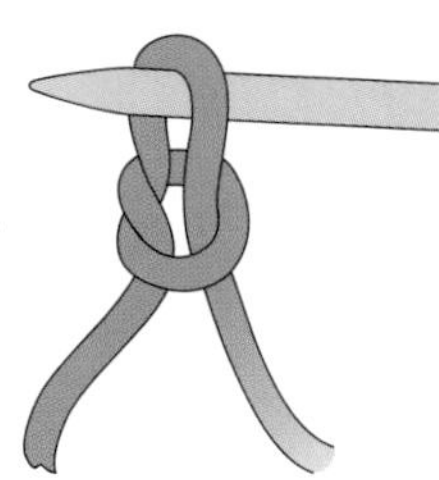

Casting on

There are several cast on methods, each with its own merits.

Thumb method

Sometimes called long-tail cast on, this uses a single needle and produces an elastic edge. It is my preferred cast on method.

1 Leaving an end about three times the length of the required cast on, put a slipknot on the needle. Holding the yarn end in the left hand, take the left thumb under the yarn and upwards. Insert the needle into the loop made on the thumb.

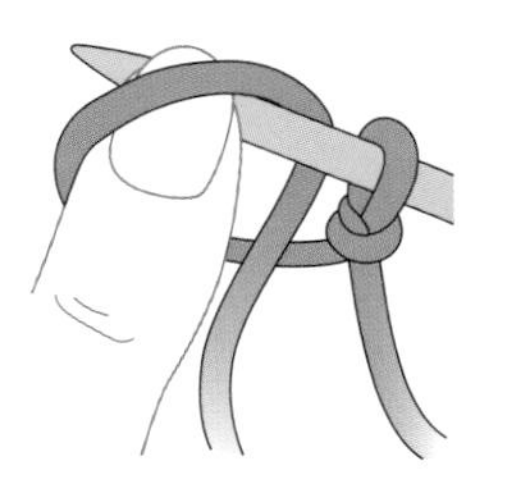

2 Use the ball end of the yarn to make a knit stitch, slipping the loop off the thumb. Pull the yarn end to close the stitch up to the needle. Continue making stitches in this way. The result looks like a row of garter stitches because the yarn has been knitted off the thumb.

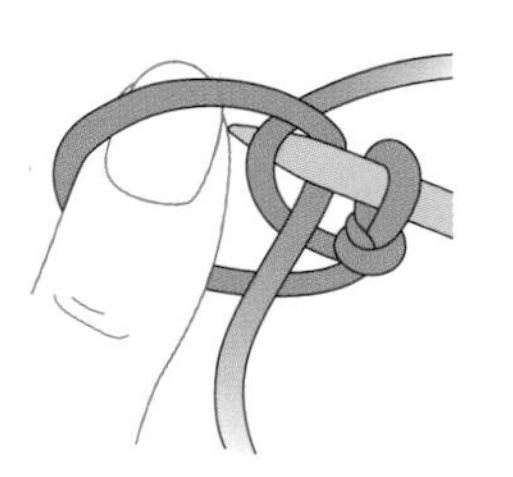

Cable cast on

This two-needle method gives a firm edge with the appearance of a rope.

1 Put a slipknot on one needle. Use the other needle and the ball end of the yarn to knit into the loop on the left-hand needle without slipping it off. Transfer the new stitch to the left-hand needle.

2 Insert the right-hand needle between the new stitch and the next stitch, and then make another stitch as before. Continue making stitches in this way.

Knitted cast on

Make a cable cast on as above, but instead of knitting between stitches, insert the right-hand needle in the front of each stitch in the usual way. This gives a softer edge than the cable method.

Knitting in the round

All of the patterns in this book involve knitting in the round on double-pointed needles. If you are accustomed to knitting in rows with a pair of needles, don't be daunted by the prospect of knitting in continuous rounds using a set of double-pointed needles. When knitting in the round using four double-pointed needles (dpns), the stitches are distributed amongst three of the needles and the spare needle is used to knit with. Many knitters prefer working in the round because of the smooth look of the finished project, as well as the reduction in pieces needing to be seamed after the knitting is done. My patterns, in particular, generally require very little (if any) seaming in order to finish the piece.

Getting started is the trickiest part, as you need to learn to hold the needles in a comfortable way, not to let the needles slip out of the stitches and not to twist the stitches of the cast on and early rounds. Remember that you will be knitting stitches from the left-hand needle onto the free needle in the usual way, and the right side (RS) will always be towards you.

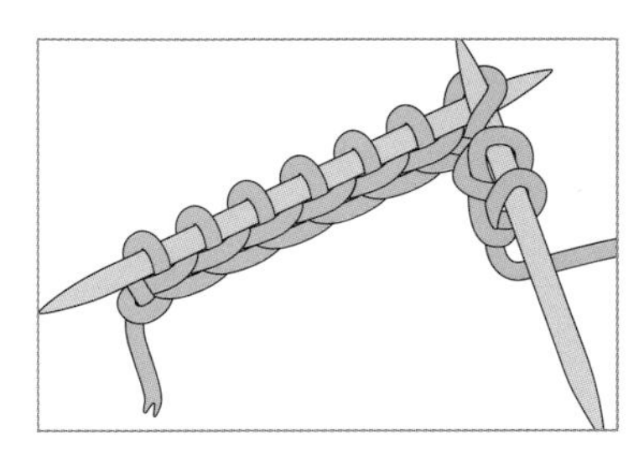

1 Using one of the methods on page 94, cast the stitches on to one needle, and from this slip the groups of stitches onto the double-pointed needles. Take care not to twist the cast on stitches as this can't be corrected later.

2 Overlapping the tips of the needles (the sequence can be changed later if necessary), arrange the needles so that the opening is towards you and the yarn is above and not below the needles.

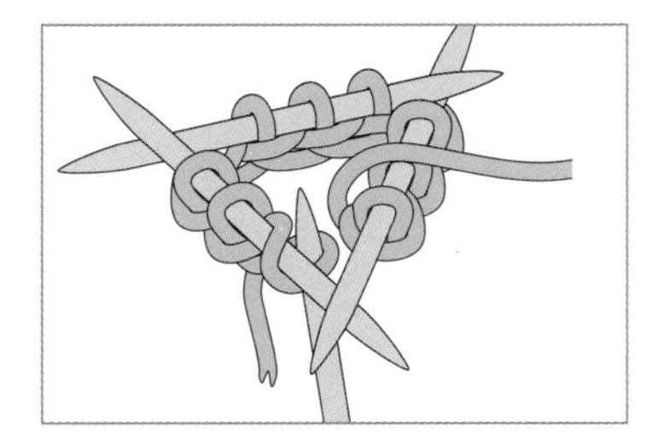

3 Join the round by working the first set of stitches with the free needle: position the needles as closely as possible and take the yarn across to make the first stitch. This should be done very firmly between needles, especially in knit rounds - otherwise a gap will appear. If the first stitch on the needle is a yarn over, this can be worked more loosely.

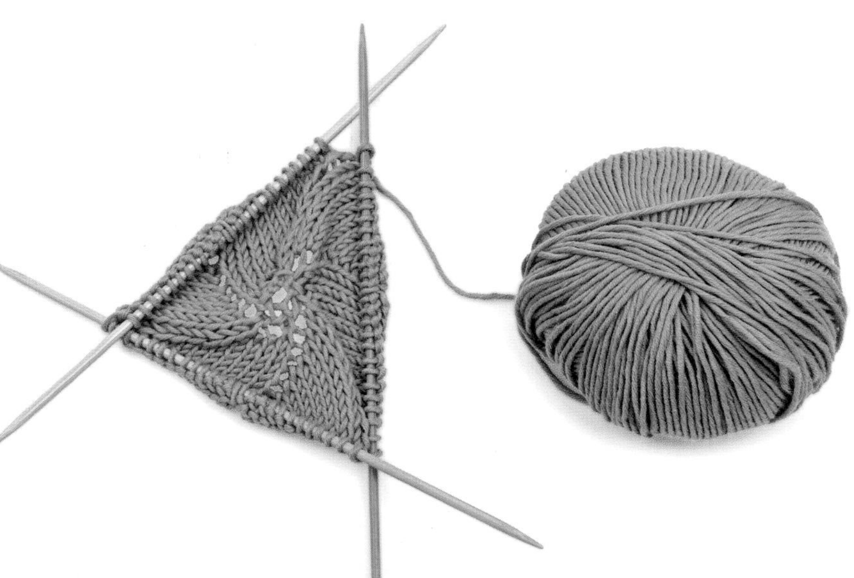

This is what some work in progress looks like when the stitches are distributed around three of a set of four double-pointed needles.

Tip Try using bamboo needles. I find that, being lighter in weight, they are less liable to slip out of the stitches.

Pick up and knit

The pick up and knit technique involves knitting up new stitches along the edge of a knitted piece, ready to work in another direction. This avoids having to cast on a separate piece and join it with a seam. Insert the right-hand needle under an edge stitch, take the yarn around the needle and pull a loop through to make a stitch. Repeat for the number of stitches required, spacing the picked-up stitches evenly along the edge. You will come across this technique in the patterns as the instruction PU.

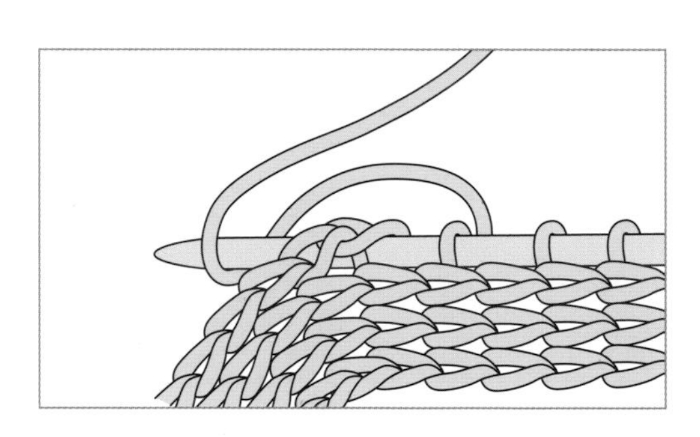

I-cord

A very useful round cord can be made using two double-pointed needles. Cast on four (or the required number of) stitches and knit one row in the usual way. *Without turning, slide the stitches to the opposite end of the needle. Take the yarn firmly across the wrong side from left to right and knit one row. Repeat from * for the required length.

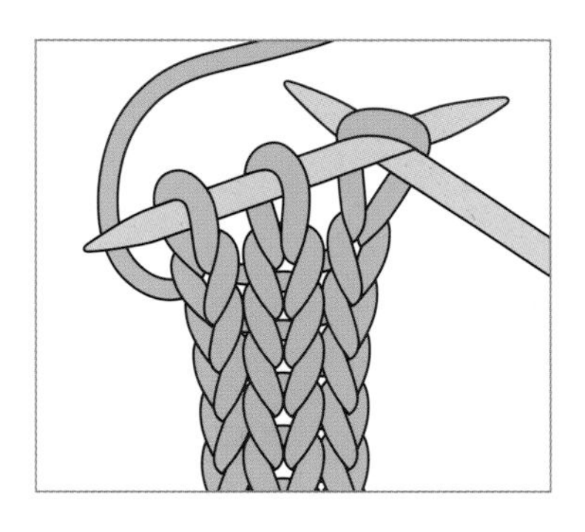

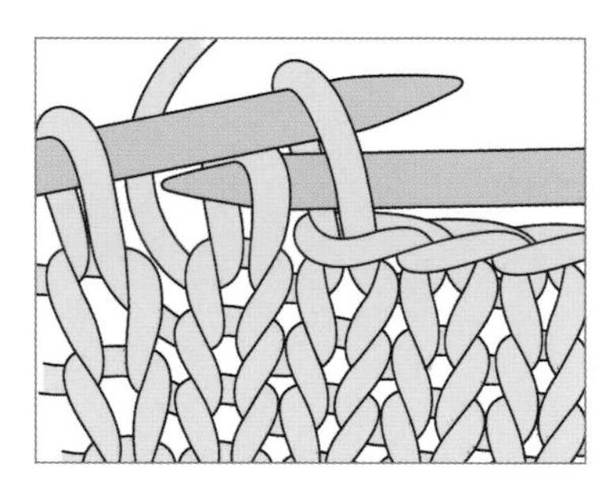

Casting and fastening off

A simple knit-stitch cast off is used in this book. Knit two stitches. *With the left-hand needle, lift the first stitch over the second and off the right-hand needle. Knit the next stitch. Repeat from * until one stitch remains. Break off the yarn, pass the end through this stitch and tighten.

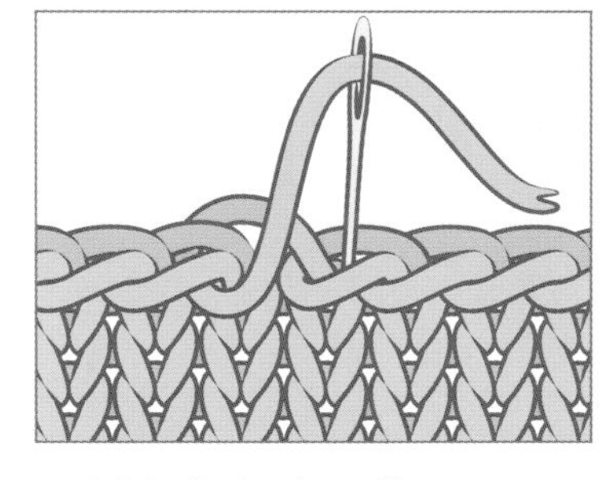

Invisible fastening off

For a smooth finish to a final round, simply break the yarn and pull it through the loop of the last stitch. Thread it onto a darning needle and take it under the two top strands of the first stitch, then back into the last stitch and pull it tight until it disappears.

ENDS

The end of yarn left after casting on or off should be a reasonable length so that it can be used to start sewing up or to cover up imperfections.

Joining new yarn inconspicuously is sometimes tricky. I prefer to leave both ends hanging slightly, tension the ends to tighten and clean up the stitches on either side and then tie a neat reef knot on the wrong side, darning in the ends later.

Wrap and turn - short rows

Short rows are used in knitting for different reasons. They can change the direction of your work, create an area of work that curves or add width to your fabric in one place, leaving the surrounding area the same.

There are different ways to work short rows, with slightly different appearances to each, but I always use the method described below - wrap and turn - which includes two wrapped stitches, one on the knit side of the fabric, and one on the purl side. You will see them in the patterns in the book described with the abbreviation wt.

Note: Wts are worked the same whether you are knitting flat or in the round.

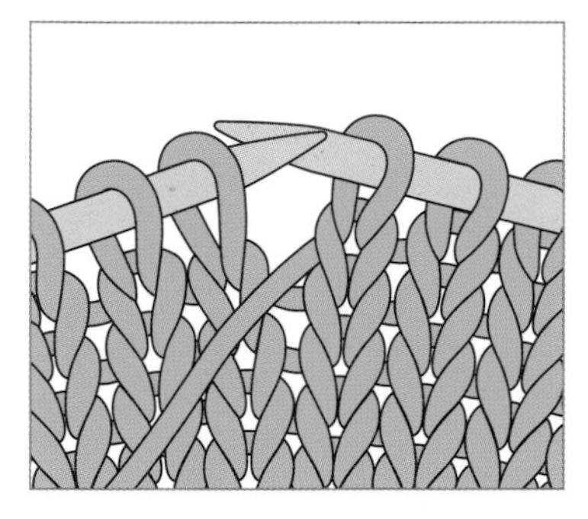

1 After knitting the specified number of stitches, bring the working yarn to the front of work.

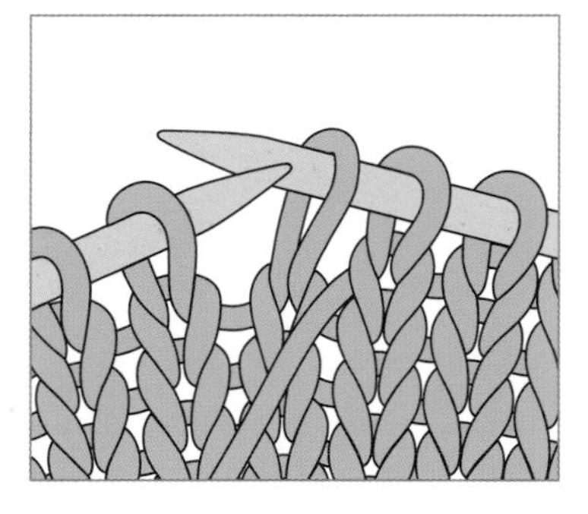

2 Slip the next stitch on the left-hand dpn purlwise to the right-hand dpn.

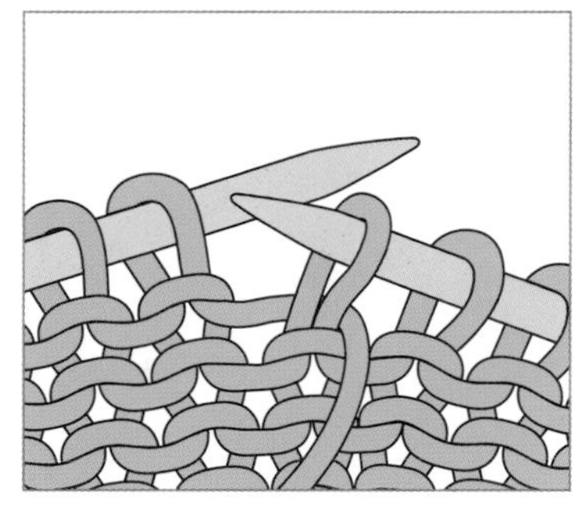

3 Move the working yarn to the back of your work, and slip the stitch back to the left-hand dpn; this wraps the first stitch. Now turn your work so that the purl side is facing you.

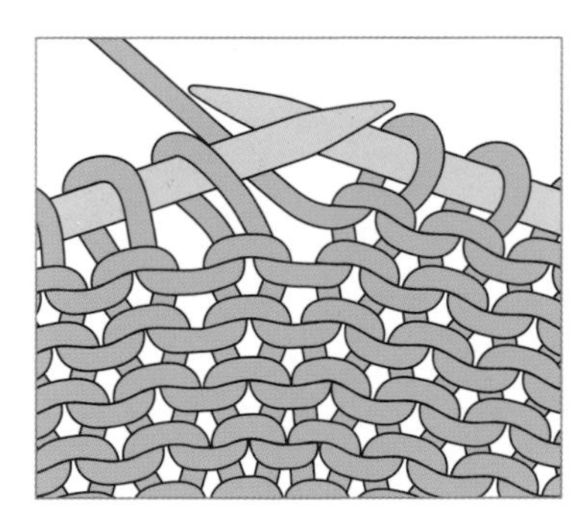

4 Purl the number of stitches indicated in the pattern, then bring the working yarn to the back of your work.

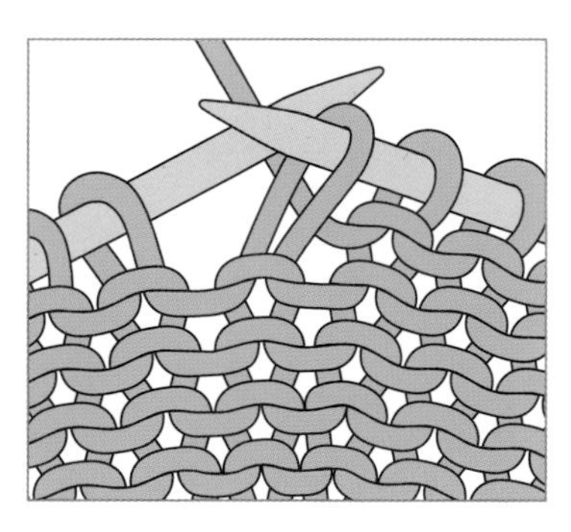

5 Slip the next stitch on the left-hand dpn purlwise to the right-hand one.

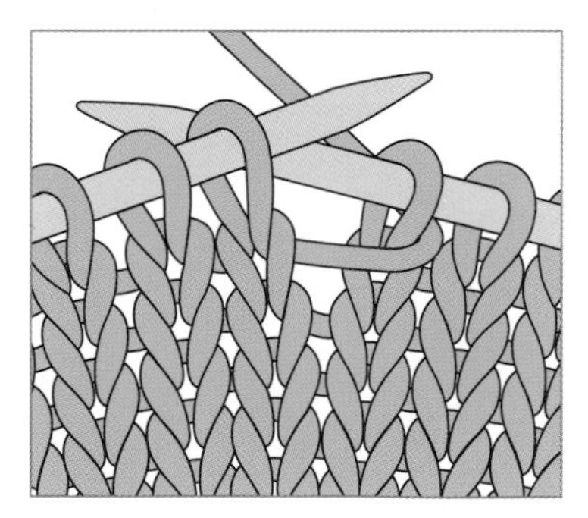

6 Bring the working yarn to the front of your work, and slip the stitch back to the left-hand dpn; this wraps the second stitch. Now turn your work so that the knit side is facing you. Finally, knit the number of stitches indicated in the pattern, which will usually bring you back to the beginning/end of the round.

Kitchener stitch

Also known as grafting, this method is used to seam two sets of live knitting invisibly with an extra row of knitting. Here we demonstrate Kitchener stitch on stocking stitch. You will need a piece of yarn (or the tail of one of your pieces), approximately three times the length of the area you want to graft, threaded onto a darning or tapestry needle.

Place your pieces with purl sides together, with the points of your needles to the right.

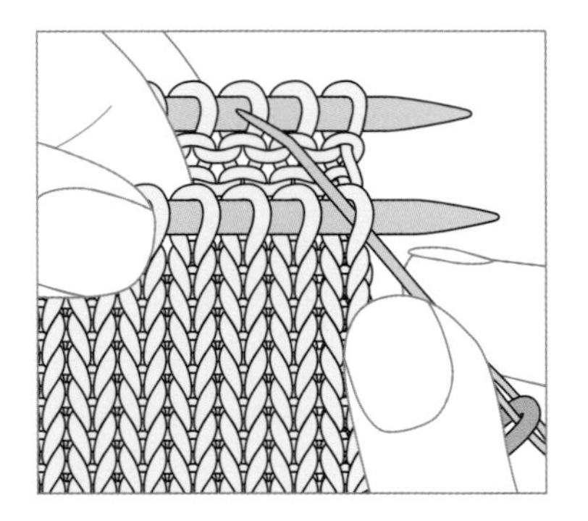

1 Insert the darning needle through the first stitch on the front needle as if to purl, and pull through. Leave the stitch on the needle.

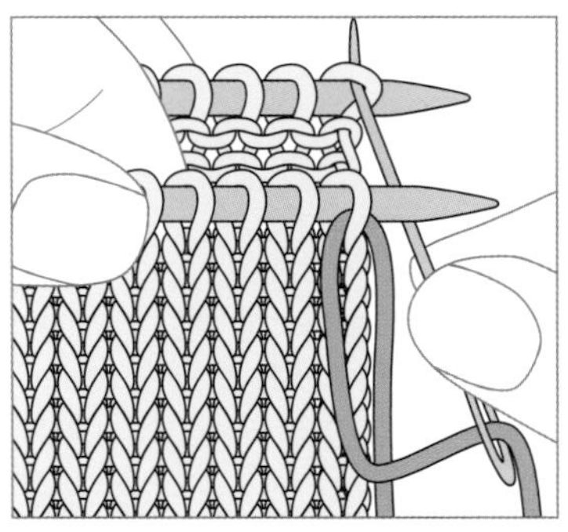

2 Insert the darning needle through the first stitch on the back needle as if to knit, and pull through. Leave the stitch on the needle.

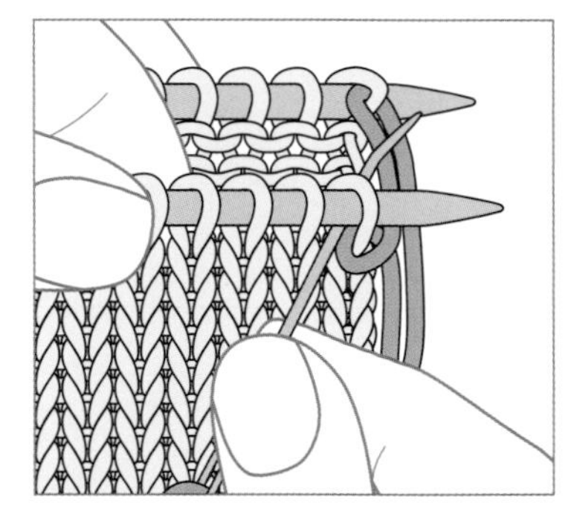

3 Insert the darning needle through the first stitch on the front needle as if to knit, and pull through. Slip this stitch off the needle.

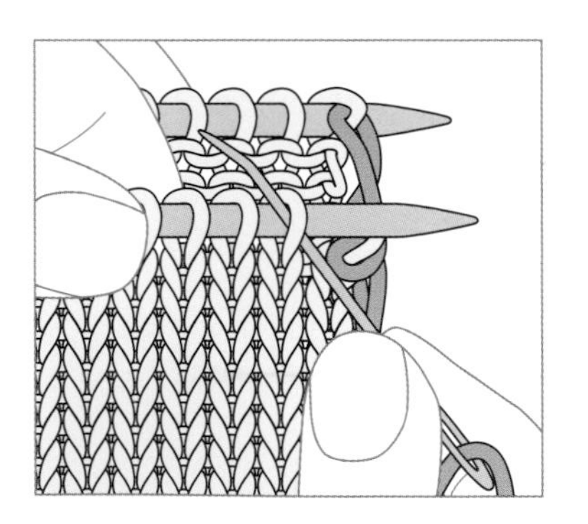

4 Insert the darning needle through the new first stitch on the front needle as if to purl, and pull through. Leave the stitch on the needle.

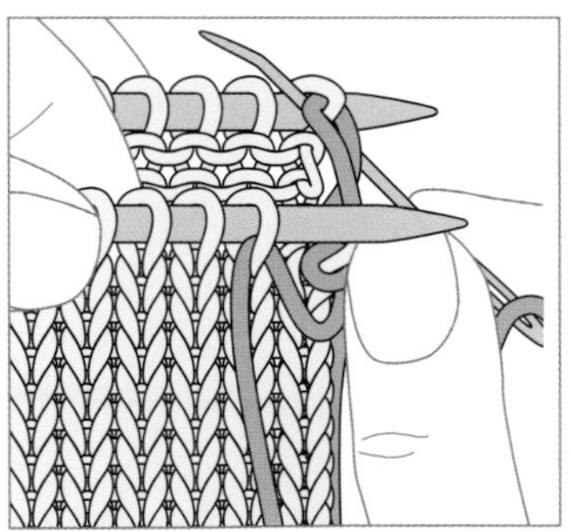

5 Insert the darning needle through the first stitch on the back needle as if to purl, and pull through. Slip this stitch off the needle.

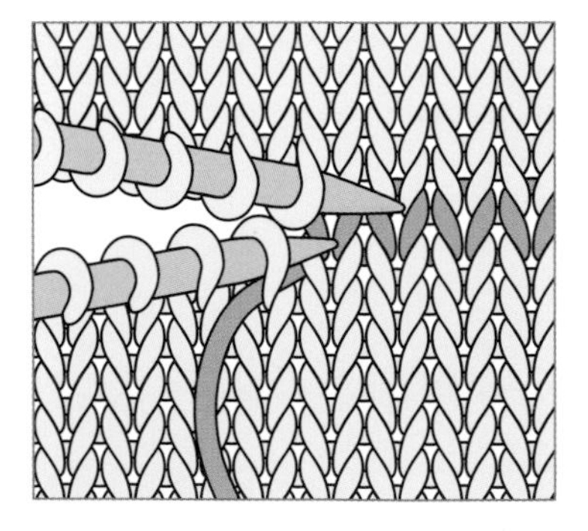

6 Insert the darning needle through the new first stitch on the back needle as if to knit, and pull through. Leave this stitch on the needle. Repeat Steps 3–6 until all the stitches have been worked.

Stuffing

I would recommend using polyester hollowfibre filling (see page 93) rather than cotton wool, as the latter can be rather dense and difficult to stitch through.

The toys in this book are all so small that you needn't worry too much about your technique when stuffing. With larger projects, you have to add the filling a tiny bit at a time, shaping as you go, but with these little cat toys, it really is just a case of grab a handful and cram it in! Remember that too much hollowfibre filling will pack down, whereas too little will never plump up. If you ever need to push the filling in somewhere your fingers can't reach, don't use a pointed implement, but use something like the rubber end of a pencil.

Weaving in ends

When working with a stuffed item, it is very simple to weave in ends. Thread any offending end onto the darning needle, and pull it into the stuffed item. Pull it back out through the other side and clip it off with scissors where it comes through the knitted fabric.

Tying off

When you are finished knitting a piece of your project, you will need to tie off the yarn. You may come across the instruction 'thread yarn through remaining live stitches, pull tight and tie off'.

1 To 'tie off', you should start by pushing your darning needle through the tiny circle and then pull the yarn until it is tight. You want the needle to come back out of the piece a few stitches below the circle. Give it a little tug to make sure that the circle is still as tight as it can be.

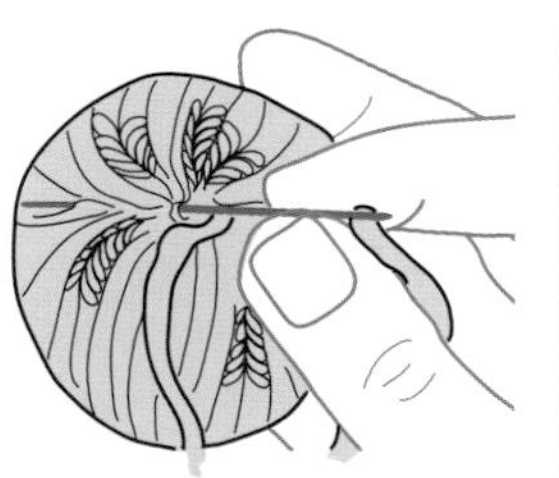

2 If you look closely at the stitches where your needle just came out, and pull them apart slightly, you will see a little bar of yarn between them. Push the tip of the needle under this bar, but do not pull it through yet.

3 Wrap the yarn around the tip of the needle twice. Pull the needle all the way through and give it a tug. The wraps you just did will form a knot.

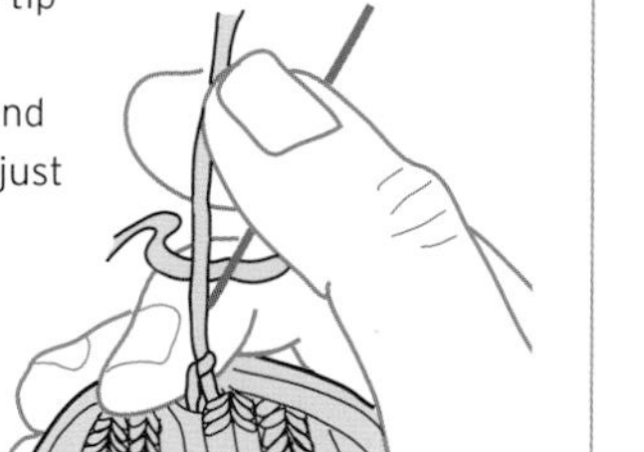

4 Push the needle back in, just above the knot, and pull back out somewhere else on the piece. This will pull the knot inside the fabric. Cut the yarn at the surface of the fabric.

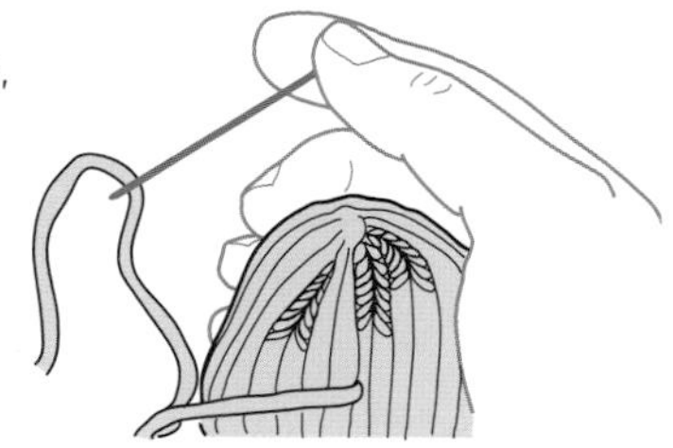

Embroidery and embellishment

On occasion, the knitted cat toys in this book have been further embellished with various decorative stitches - to add eyes or mouths - or additional elements such as antennae or legs. To help you re-create these effects, here are some simple techniques.

Embroidery stitches

Before beginning your embroidery you need to secure the thread. This can be done with a double stitch on the reverse of the piece. The tail of the thread can be woven in the back of the row.

When stitching on knitted fabric, make sure the needle is worked into the gaps between stitches so the yarn does not split.

Running stitch

This is the most basic embroidery stitch. It is very simple to do and can look very effective on a knitted fabric if used in the right way.

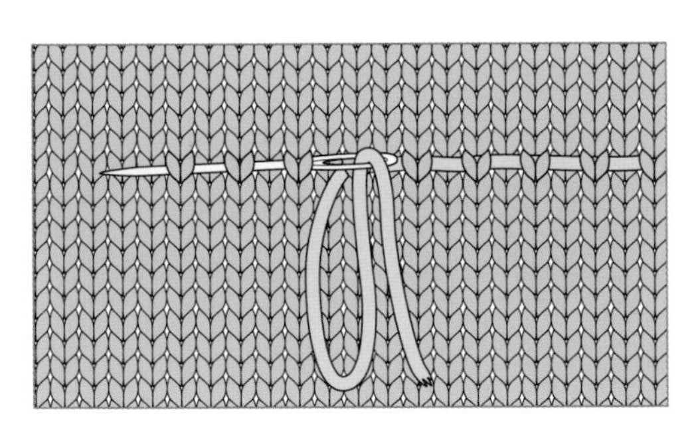

Bring the needle through from the back of the work, then insert it through the piece from front to back a short distance to the left. Bring the needle through from back to front again, a short distance to the left, ensuring that the stitches are of similar size.

Backstitch

This stitch is a good stitch for creating outlining and lines, such as a smiling mouth.

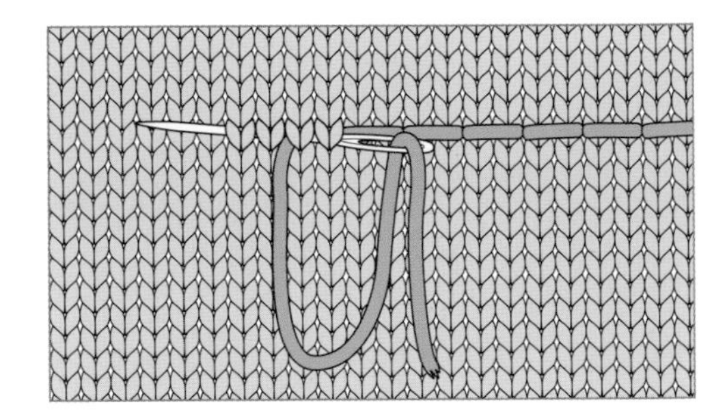

Bring the needle through from the back of the work. From the front and in one motion, take the needle through to the back a short distance along to the right, then draw back through the work to the front the same distance along to the left from the beginning of the stitch

Continue from right to left by inserting the needle through from front to back at the point where the last stitch emerged.

Satin stitch

Satin stitch is a very firm embroidery method and is used to completely cover the knitted stitches. It is a good stitch for embroidering larger eyes, Teddy's nose or perhaps the spots on Miss Ladybird's back.

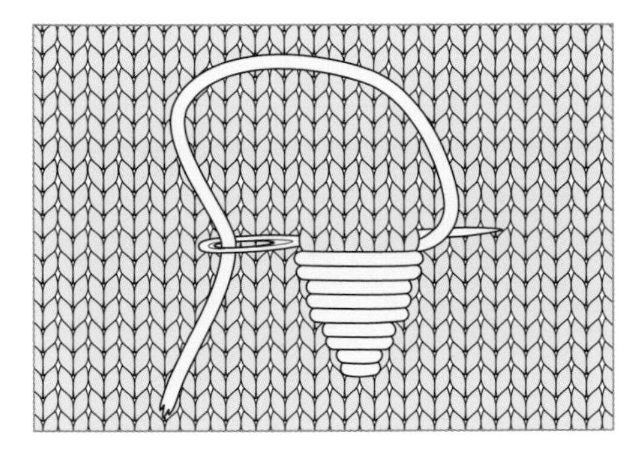

Make small stitches at a slight angle as close together as possible, by bringing the yarn through from the back and then from front to back the required distance away.

French knots

Making a nice, round knot is a useful surface decoration that just needs a little practice. This is great for adding eyes and noses to your toys.

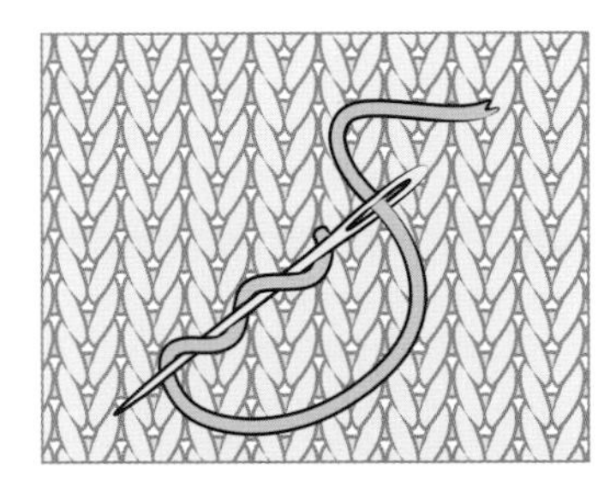

1 Hold the yarn down with the left thumb and twist the darning needle twice around the taut yarn. For a larger knot, make an additional twist.

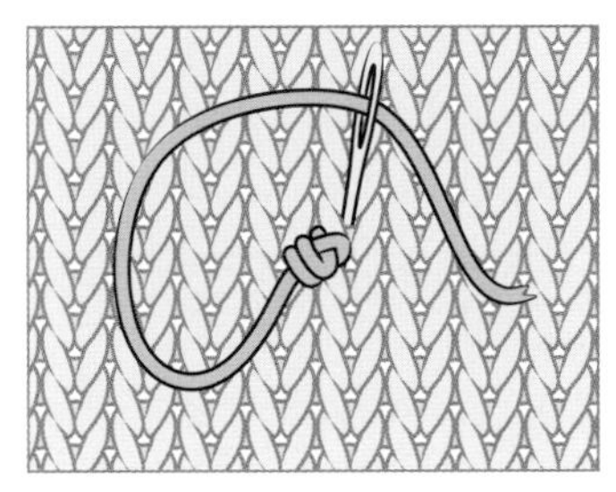

2 Still holding the yarn, pull the needle through the twists, insert it in the same place in the knitting, and pull it through to the WS (wrong side).

Duplicate stitch

This technique, sometimes called Swiss darning, is used to make colour changes or additions to an area of stocking stitch. The new colour covers the stitches exactly but adds to the thickness of the fabric, so it's better only used over small areas. Use a darning needle with a rounded point and work from right to left horizontally and from bottom to top vertically.

Working to the left

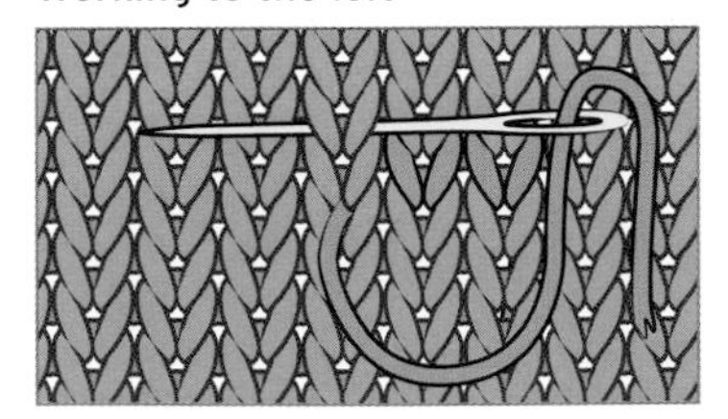

1 Thread the contrast colour onto a darning needle, bring it out at the base of one v-shaped stitch, take it behind the two threads of the stitch above and bring it out at the front.

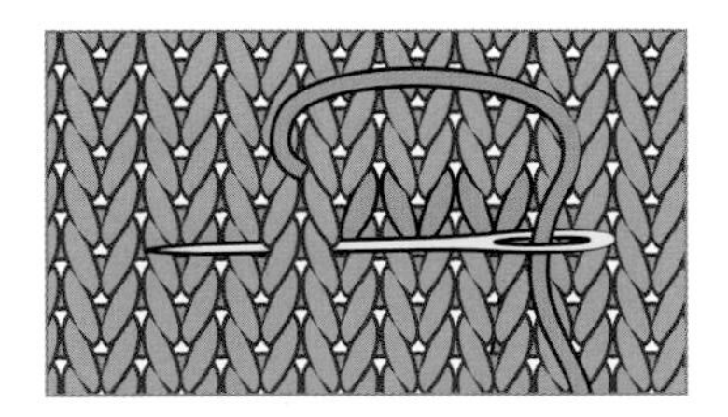

2 Tensioning the yarn carefully, insert the darning needle into the base of the stitch and bring it out at the base of the next stitch.

Working upwards

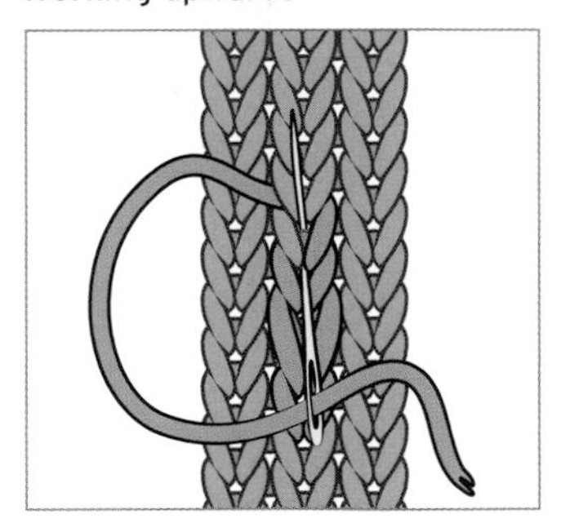

Using a darning needle, cover a stitch as in Step 1 of working to the left, but bring the needle out in the stitch above. Over a large number of rows miss one stitch at regular intervals or the work will buckle.

Additional embellishments

In many of the patterns in this book, additional elements have been added, such as legs and antennae, after the main shape of the toy has been knitted. These finishing touches look great and really bring the toys to life. They're all added in the same way, with just a darning needle and a small amount of yarn. It couldn't be simpler.

First, take a strand of yarn longer than the desired length for the leg or antenna and thread it onto a darning needle.

Secure the yarn on the inside of your work by any method that works for you. You can either make a knot at the end of the yarn which, when pulled through the fabric and inside of the stuffing, will catch. Or, insert your darning needle into a discreet place on the body (like the bottom), and make a couple of tiny stitches. Choose whichever method you'd like, then draw the needle out in the place where you would like to position the leg or antenna and cut the yarn at the desired length. Simple as that!

You can use this exact same technique for attaching a long strand of yarn to the top of any of the toys in the book. This will allow you to play with your kitty by dangling the toy in front of her. Your cat will most likely love leaping and jumping for any of the toys in the book, but this looks particularly effective to human eyes on those 'flying' projects, such as Bye-bye birdie, Dragonfly drop and Butterfly kisses.

Tip Don't feel you need to stick to exactly what you see in the book, but use it as a guideline; a starting point. You can let your imagination loose and add any embellishments you can think of: feathers, bells, pompoms, ribbons - trust me, your cat will love them all!

Essential stitches

Even if you're already a proficient knitter, it never hurts to have a reminder of the basics to hand. Here you'll find a cheat sheet for all the basic knit stitches you'll encounter in this book.

Knit (k)

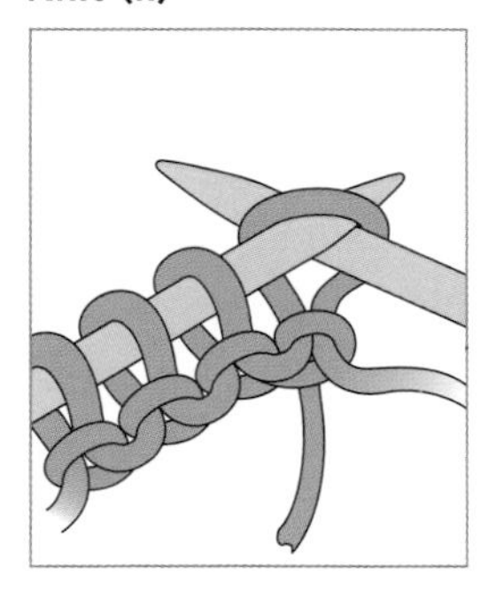

1 Insert the right-hand needle into the first stitch on the left-hand needle. Make sure it goes from left to right into the front of the stitch.

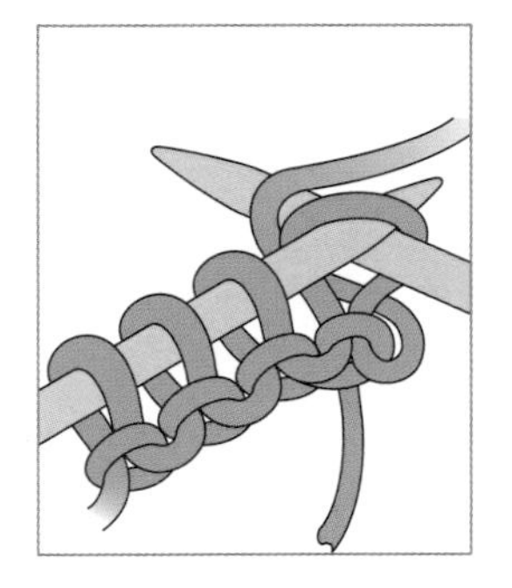

2 Taking the yarn behind, bring it up and around the right-hand needle clockwise.

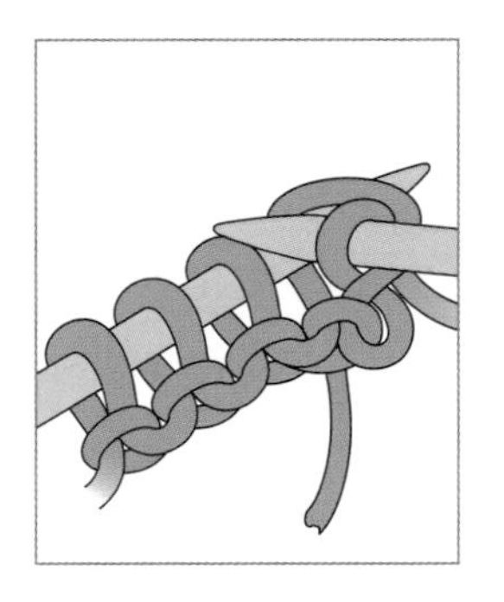

3 Using the tip of the right-hand needle, draw a loop of the working yarn through the stitch.

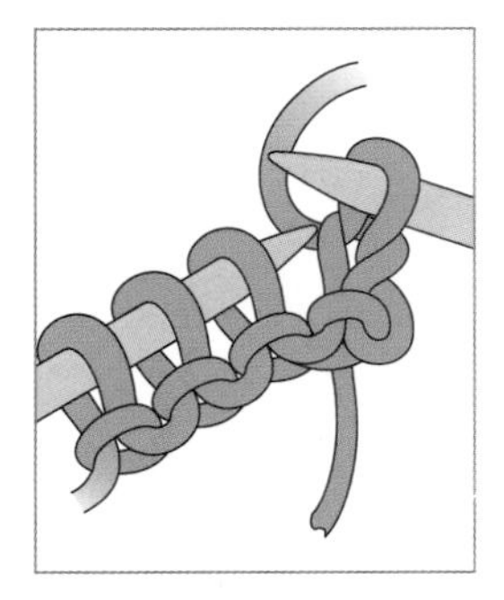

4 Slip the stitch off the left-hand needle. There is now a new stitch on the right-hand needle.

Purl (p)

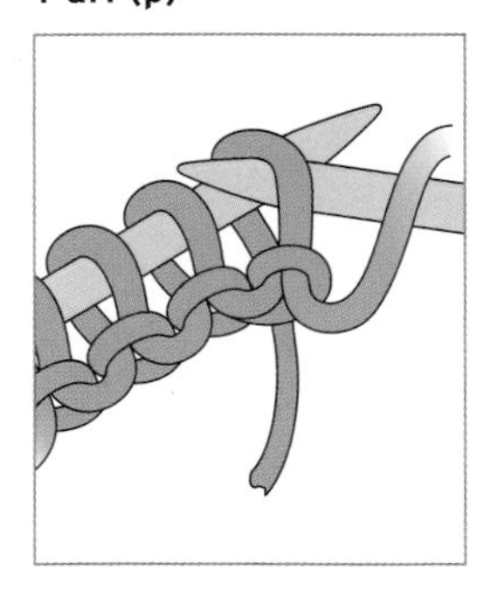

1 Insert the right-hand needle into the first stitch on the left-hand needle. Make sure it goes into the stitch from right to left up into the front of the stitch.

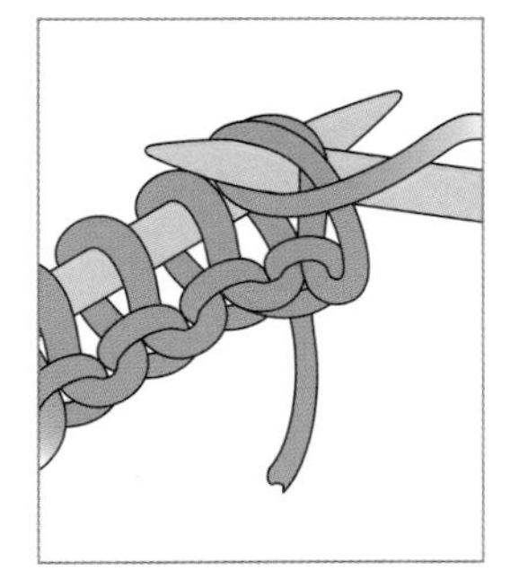

2 Bringing the yarn to the front, loop it around the right-hand needle anticlockwise.

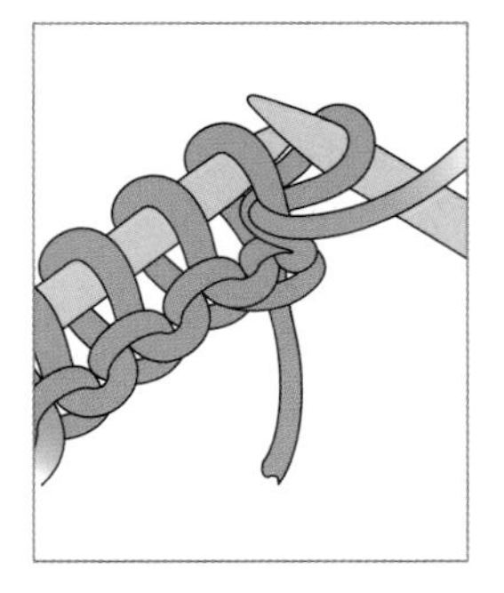

3 Lower the tip of the right-hand needle, taking it away from you to draw a loop of the working yarn through the stitch.

4 Slip the stitch off the left-hand needle. There is now a new stitch on the right-hand needle.

Decreases

Right-slanting single decrease (k2tog)

Knitting two stitches together makes a smooth shaping, with the second stitch lying on top of the first. You can purl two stitches together (p2tog) by inserting the needle into the stitches from right to left and completing like a normal purl stitch (see page 103).

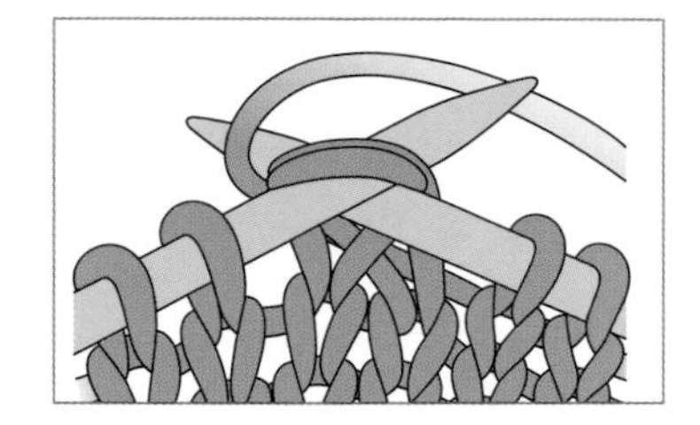

1 Insert the right-hand needle through the front of the first two stitches on the left-hand needle, then loop the yarn around the needle.

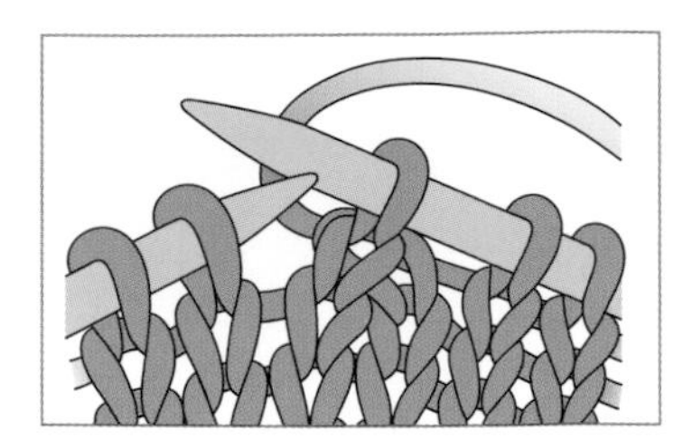

2 Draw the loop through and drop the two stitches off the left-hand needle. One stitch decreased.

Left-slanting single decrease (ssk)

This particular decrease technique has a left-leaning slant.

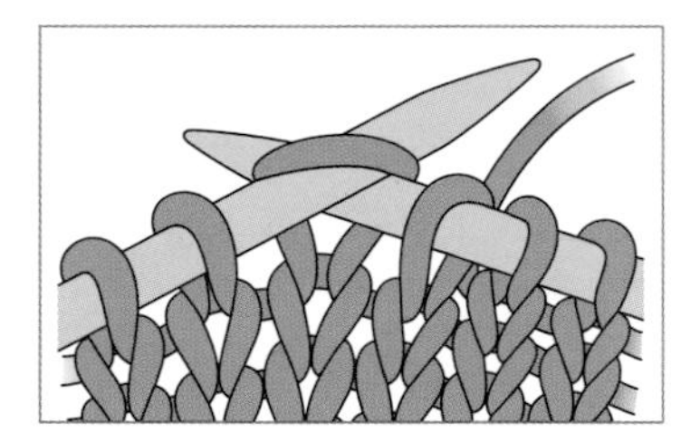

1 Insert the right-hand needle knitwise (as if to knit the next stitch) through the front of the next stitch on the left-hand needle, and slip it onto the right. Repeat for the next stitch.

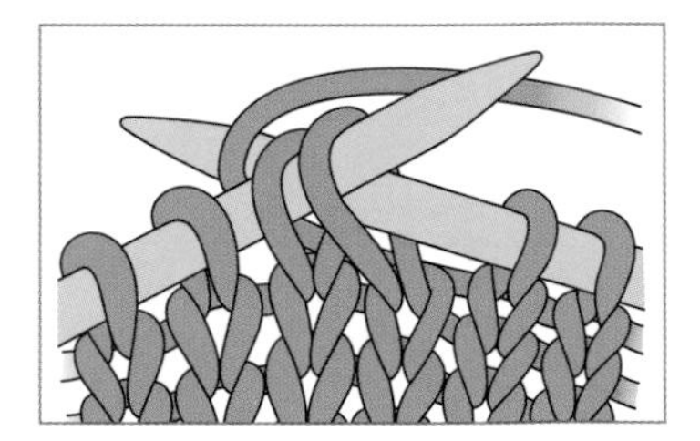

2 Insert the left-hand needle into the front of these two stitches and knit them together. One stitch decreased.

Increases

Bar increase on a knit row (kfb)

Knitting into the front and the back of a stitch is the most common increase. It's a neat, firm increase, which makes a little bar on the right side of the work at the base of the new stitch and doesn't leave a hole.

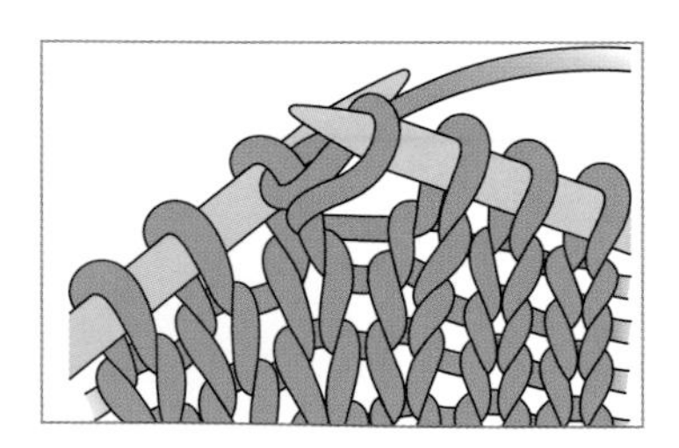

1 Knit into the front of the stitch and pull the loop through, but leave the stitch on the left-hand needle.

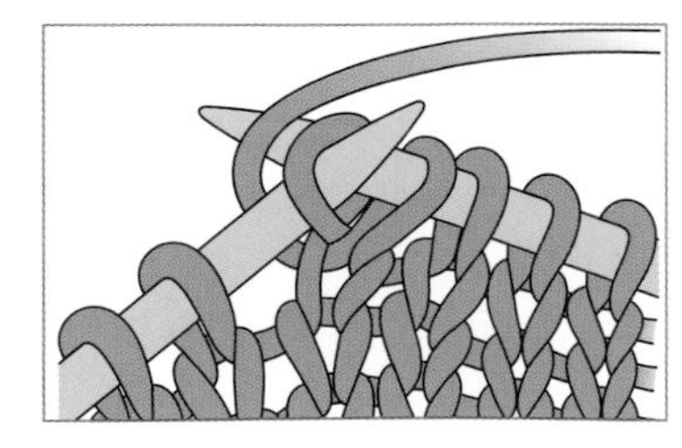

2 Knit into the back of the stitch on the left-hand needle.

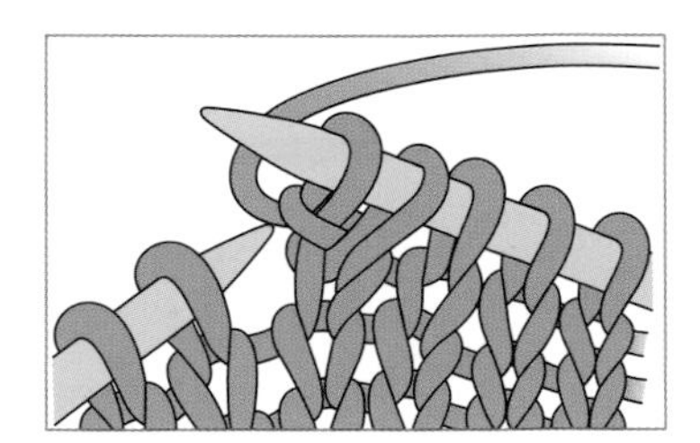

3 Slip the stitch off the left-hand needle, making two stitches on the right-hand needle. Note that the bar of the new stitch lies on the left.

Make one (M1)

Making a stitch from the strand between stitches is a very neat way to increase. Here we look at two methods for doing this - use whichever you prefer.

Method 1 (this is my preferred method)

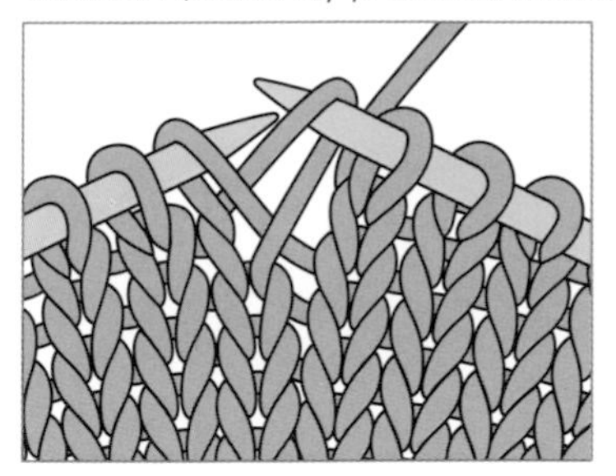

1 Insert the tip of the right-hand needle from front to back going under the right leg of the stitch directly below the next stitch to be worked.

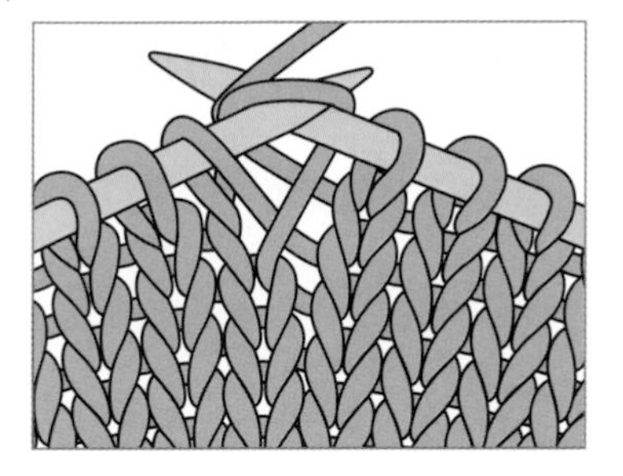

2 Place this onto the left-hand needle and knit into this loop as you would any other stitch. Knit the next stitch as usual.

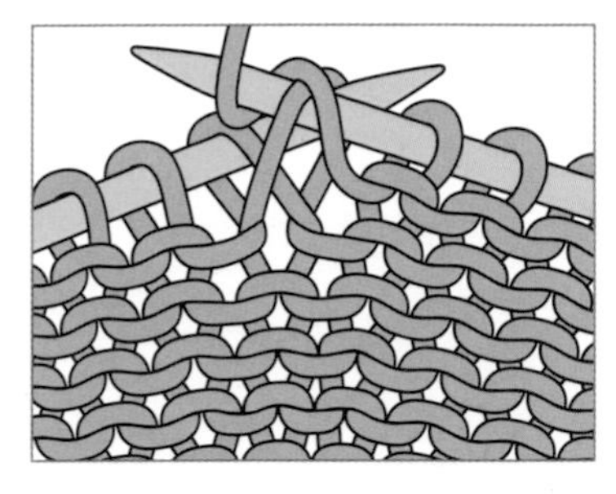

To M1p (make 1 purlwise), with the yarn to the front, use the right-hand needle to lift up the purl bump of the stitch below the stitch about to be worked. Transfer to the left-hand needle and purl as usual.

Method 2

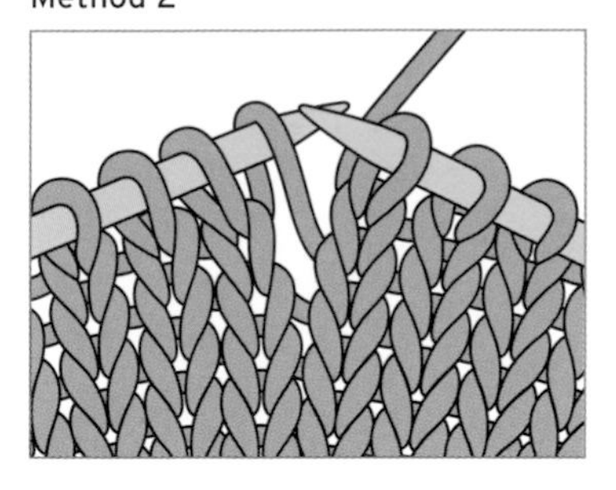

1 Insert the tip of the left-hand needle from front to back under the connecting yarn between the stitches on the left-hand and right-hand needles.

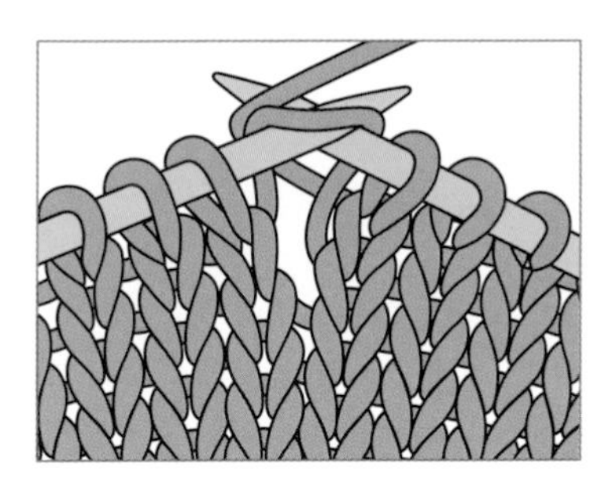

2 Insert the tip of the right-hand needle from front to back into the front of the loop you have just put onto the left-hand needle. Knit this stitch.

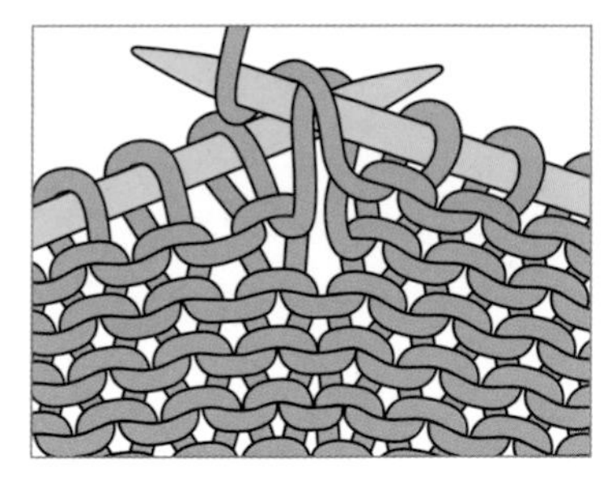

To M1p (make 1 purlwise), with the yarn to the front, insert the left-hand needle from back to front under the strand between the left-hand and right-hand needles. Hold the loop on the left-hand needle. Insert the right-hand needle tip up into the front of the loop on the left-hand needle and purl this stitch.

Meet the cats

We would like to say a huge thank you to our feline friends and their human families for helping with the book.

The Models

Annelis (Silver Spotted British Shorthair), courtesy of Susan Marchant, featured on page 29.

Beemo, courtesy of Fiona Brandford, featured on pages 61-62.

Belle (Silver Tabby British Shorthair), courtesy of Susan Marchant, featured on pages 26, 57, 58 and 79-81.

Charlie-Girl (Black and white crossbreed), courtesy of Jane Harrison, featured on page 51.

Gracie (Maine Coon), courtesy of Clare Earthey, featured on page 14.

Gunter (Black Smoke Norwegian Forest Cat), courtesy of Yufan Chen, featured on pages 48-49 and 87.

Holly (Maine Coon), courtesy of Clare Earthey, featured on pages 36-37 and 42.

Huckleberry (Maine Coon), courtesy of Clare Earthey, featured on pages 20-21 and 74.

Little H (Maine Coon), courtesy of Clare Earthey, featured on pages 2, 69, 83 and 89.

Lorelei (Semi-longhair Tortoiseshell tabby crossbreed), courtesy of Jane Harrison, featured on pages 32 and 46-47.

Luna (Oriental), courtesy of Daniel Burn, featured on page 55 (right).

Luna (Snow Bengal cross), courtesy of Alix Taylor, featured on pages 10 and 12 (right).

Mooch (British Shorthair with Siamese points), courtesy of Simone Hogan, featured on pages 22-23, 41, 66 and 84.

Orphelia (Silver Spotted British Shorthair), courtesy of Susan Marchant, featured on page 28.

Rigby, courtesy of Fiona Brandford, featured on pages 31 and 63.

Tilly, courtesy of Melissa Quinley, featured on page 86 (see page 107 for photo).

Tuna, courtesy of Lindy Zubairy, featured on pages 33, 71-73 and 77.

Vivi (Abyssinian), courtesy of Alix Taylor, featured on pages 12, 24 (left), 34-35, 38, 44-45, 64 and 88.

Ziggy (Oriental), courtesy of Daniel Burn, featured on pages 1, 3, 16, 19, 43, 52-54, 55 (left) and 109.

The Test Cats

To make sure that your cats will love playing with the toys in this book, we asked some cats we know to test them out and give them their seal of approval. Thank you to our test cats (and to their owners, who kindly tested the knitting patterns).

Angelina and **Riley** (and their owner, Stefanie Freeman)

Artie (and owner Aldona Shumway)

Artemis (and owner Vivian Lee)

Austin and **Gideon** (and their owner, Amy Hedgecoke)

Brigid and **Fergus** (and their owner, Claire Piper)

Charlie (and owner Petrina Rooney)

Diablo and **Kopper** (and their owner, Jennifer Hood)

Faith (and owner Lorysa Cornish)

Greeley (and owner Joanne Thomas)

Madame Mim (and owner Gabriele)

Michael (and owner Karen Woodie)

Ming (and owner Karen)

Missy (and owner Teresa Morneau)

Olivia and **Morris** (and their owner, Rosemary Chapman)

Patch (and owner Emily Parkerson)

Sprite and **Whisk** (and their owner, Kristin Murray)

Stormy (and owner Kendise Dunn)

Tilly (and test knitter Ann Silberlicht)

Riley

Madame Mim

Missy

Tilly

Whisk

Artemis

Michael

Austin and Gideon

Abbreviations

CO cast on

Dpn(s) double-pointed needle(s)

K knit

K2tog knit 2 sts together

Kfb knit in front and back of one st

Kfbf knit in front, back and front of one st

Kfbfbf knit in front, back, front, back and front of one st

M1 make one st

M1p make one st purlwise

MB make bobble

P purl

P2tog purl 2 sts together

PU pick up and knit

RS right side

Sl slip

Ssk slip, slip, knit

St(s) stitch(es)

WS wrong side

Wt wrap and turn

INDEX